Landscape Architecture
on Global Terrain

HATJE
CANTZ

A.M.

out there

Landscape Architecture
on Global Terrain

This book is published in
conjunction with
the exhibition by the
Architekturmuseum
der TU München,
Pinakothek der Moderne
April 27 – August 20, 2017

Edited by Andres Lepik in
cooperation with Undine
Giseke, Regine Keller, Jörg
Rekittke, Antje Stokman,
and Chiristian Werthmann

out there

Landscape Architecture
on Global Terrain

Contents

Andres Lepik

Preface

At the beginning of the twenty-first century, planet Earth finds itself in an increasingly critical situation, since humankind is in the process of ultimately destroying its own habitat with all the means available to it. And it is doing so with full awareness, having long recognized the warning signs: climate change, the melting of the poles, flooding catastrophes, species extinction. Forty-five years after the publication of *The Limits to Growth,* the pioneering book by the Club of Rome, this situation has barely changed, while political structures have adapted to the situation in only a few cases. But the battle over the distribution of the resources that remain has become relentless. "America first" is the most recent and cynical slogan for a national egoism that does not want to apprehend that humankind as a whole bears responsibility and must act together since there are no replacement planets, even for those who deny the facts.

In light of these developments, the term "landscape" has also arrived at a turning point, above all when we understand this term to mean the popular notion of a locus amoenus as an aesthetic category. Ultimately, every landscape is now directly dependent on the processes that accompany the increase in the human population and its growing needs. And landscape architecture must focus more and more on the systems that will determine our life contexts in the future. Depicting and analyzing specific situations is the first step toward facilitating responsible action, toward developing tools with which landscape in the future can still be designed in a sensible way in the first place, meaning in relation to ever further deteriorating general conditions. It is crucial to aim for broad attention to the complex systems in which we are meanwhile all accomplices and victims at the same time. Whether the problems that are recognized and described will lead to short- or long-term "solutions" is therefore perhaps even secondary.

Since 2013,
the Architekturmuseum der Technischen
Universität München (Architecture Museum
of the Technical University in Munich) has
intensively dedicated itself in its program
to questions regarding the social relevance
of planning and building in a global context.
With the exhibition *out there—Landscape
Architecture on Global Terrain,* we are for
the first time now also presenting landscape
architecture, a discipline that has already
been part of the Faculty for Architecture of
our university for many years. The project
arose from a joint initiative of five universities whose research is devoted to spaces that
stand exemplarily for the current condition-
ality of humankind in the twenty-first century.
They are megacities or other municipalities
whose material cycles and processes of
growth are having more and more consequences for the provisioning, safety, and
economic opportunities of millions of people.
Ten projects and analyses make exemplary
situations visible and, in some cases, also
offer alternative courses of action. We hope
that this exhibition will also make it clear to
a broader public what a special role landscape architecture can have for global
developments.

Undine Giseke, Regine Keller, Jörg Rekittke, Antje Stokman, Christian Werthmann

Out There

Landscape Architecture on Global Terrain

Landscape architecture is a relatively young academic discipline. The driving force behind its establishment and the development of a specific spectrum of tasks emerged in the context of a rapidly urbanizing and industrializing Europe at the end of the nineteenth century where a striking lack of public urban space was available for civic use. In line with modernism and its paradigm of technical feasibility, the discipline has again and again been faced with calls to improve the urban environment, be it through facilitating a healthier way of life more closely connected to nature, through promoting socially just access to urban green spaces, or simply through the cosmetic beautification of cities.

As a result, the broader public overwhelmingly perceives landscape architects primarily as positive figures—who make cities green and hence stand in sharp contrast to architects, who are generally associated with urban concrete. This notion is reinforced by numerous actors in the field of landscape architecture who identify as landscape gardeners, claiming that they work with beauty, and who aspire to be regarded as artists through creating anthropogenic nature.

The authors of this exhibition are not interested in any of these classical roles. Their works do not represent any of the abovementioned promises of salvation. Individuals who expect landscape architects to design urban paradises in the form of gardens and parks, to bring green to cities, streets, and squares, and to strive to beautify the world will be disappointed by this exhibition. In this case, a conscious decision was made to not attempt to equate landscape architecture with the professional fields of garden and landscape construction, garden maintenance and conservation, or with the historical subject of garden art.

The focus of this exhibition and catalogue is on approaches and working methods that distance landscape architecture from the clichés of the green, the beautiful, and the serene. They deal with a global reality that is becoming, in an increasingly drastic way, neither green nor beautiful and for many populations, difficult to bear. In countries where cities are growing more rapidly than ever, one sees an urbanity that is frequently uninviting, brutal, dirty, merciless, and shamelessly harmful to the environment. It is not possible to come to terms with this contemporary version of global urbanization through Western-style civic green spaces and bureaucratically mandated green area quotas, or with the promise of paradise inherent in them. The virulence of rapidly growing cities gives rise to diverse and multifaceted problems and with them, new approaches to transformation need to be developed. These new nodal points of urbanization are active generators of knowledge concerning the future of cities and how they are connected to the natural environment. With these emerging trends, the tasks of the professional fields of planners, architects, and landscape architects have also inevitably expanded.

It has become clear that landscape and city are two complex and constantly interacting systems that frequently give rise to conflicts. Landscape has long since ceased being a world alternative to the city. Landscape is not what is "outside," even though this simple picture still has an undeniable allure. Landscape is rather the substance, the recipient, and the trigger of huge urban processes and a basis of urban metabolism. The city constantly channels into itself commodities and natural resources—produced in near or far-flung landscapes—and much too frequently discharges them undigested back into the landscape in the form of rubbish and wastewater. Both spatial phenomena are very closely interwoven—morphologically and materially, socially and economically—and their boundaries are becoming more and more fluid. The city is in the landscape, and the landscape is in the city. Their intertwining and coexistence are synergetic, but at the same time also inharmonious and conflict-laden. Specifically this means dealing with the destruction of cultural landscapes as well as with flooding, landslides, garbage mountains or earthquakes in cities, and the growing city's enormous demand for space, food, and water. It then becomes clear that the urban system, with its diverse interdependencies, is difficult to manage. Like the impenetrable primeval landscapes of the past, today it is the newly emerging urban landscapes that represent a kind of new terra incognita as a result of their complexity, boundlessness, and sheer size.

Despite the availability of high-resolution satellite images, we are faced with new mysteries. In a highly cross-linked world, everything seems to be interconnected, yet still cannot be grasped in all of its complexity. As landscape architects, we also see it as our responsibility to deal with very concrete localities, for instance, with steep but densely settled slopes at risk of landslides, where people, animals, and plants have to try to coexist with one another—or quite simply to survive. For us, landscape architecture means acquiring concrete, site-specific competence through closely observing and deciphering the various urban-natural interdependencies as well as possible. Though this might also be achieved with a view from the outside, identifying parameters that might serve as the basis for change processes necessitates not only being on-site, but also being involved in the location in order to cooperate with stakeholders, to imagine concrete changes, and to initiate actions.

The projects in this catalogue are therefore dedicated first and foremost to understanding the interdependencies of city and landscape along with their complicated coexistence. The attendant problems can be seen more drastically than anywhere else in the urbanization processes currently taking place mostly outside of Europe. This is the reason why the field of activity of the participants in this exhibition is situated outside their home countries. What all of them share is their German origin and their internationally oriented academic teaching and research. What the project sites have in common, on the other hand, are the scale of their landscape-related challenges and the fact that the profession of landscape architecture in these locations has largely been lacking up to now. The exhibition can therefore be understood as a report on how European landscape architects address the challenges of the globalization of their fields of work, how they work in diverse cultural contexts—out there—with whom and how they cooperate, and what new knowledge can emerge through such cooperation. With all the baggage of the legacy of Western colonialism, this also means working together in ways that are sensitive to this history.

The ten projects presented here deal with different experimental approaches on various continents. Having been developed within the university context, the works show how contemporary landscape architecture proceeds in identifying and tackling the multilayered, immense, and frequently intractable problems of the respective locations.

The individual projects counter the familiar image of the creative genius who approaches problems in a jaunty manner and who offers solutions based on his or her own personal design approach, advocating instead the research-oriented exploration of interrelationships and interactions, as well as the identification of starting points for spatial interventions. This results in concepts where the processes and stakeholders determine the contents, and not the contents the processes. Such an approach consciously risks being open-ended, and bids farewell to the idea of offering perfect solutions.

This might be unusual for a profession that has traditionally earned its income through developing specific solutions and implementing them as built projects. To escape the automatism of professional and cultural conditioning, the authors take a step back, and adopt appropriate tools from related disciplines such as ethnography, anthropology, and geography. They work in interdisciplinary teams in cooperation with geologists, climatologists, sociologists, water resource management experts, agronomists, traffic planners, and economists, so as to develop integrated solutions that combine the knowledge of various specialist disciplines together in a novel way. They develop approaches to solutions in cooperation with local stakeholders. The individual projects strive to explore different approaches to ascertaining the respective linkages of city and landscape, to set various priorities depending on the particular situation, and to occupy themselves with plausible forms of future coexistence.

In Casablanca and Kigali, the focus is on the urbanizing region as a whole. A growing sensitivity to the question of how cities are supplied with food opens up new perspectives on urban landscapes. Their productive side becomes the starting point for contemplating future production chains and for concretely initiating a stronger linkage of material flows between urban and rural spheres by means of new stakeholder networks.

Climate change and rapid urbanization are resulting in an increasing scarcity of water resources worldwide and in the pollution of natural bodies of water.

Changde and Lima are reference cities in which it is shown, based on the circulation of water, how it is possible to develop and implement strategies that focus on a productive interplay between natural ecosystems, technical infrastructure, and human lifestyles in a way that is adapted to the conditions of the local natural surroundings and their respective cultural contexts.

The case studies in Medellín and São Paulo examine natural hazards such as landslides and flooding, which, heightened by progressive global warming, predominantly affect the lowest income groups in global urbanization. The feasibility of developing—as a result of the shared threat—collaborative landscape strategies that offer those affected an improvement in their overall living situation is explored based on specific examples.

The peripheral neighborhoods of Cañada Real Galiana in Madrid and the district of Canaan near Port-au-Prince, Haiti, are characterized as informal settlements, which first have to be understood in their particularities in order to then develop with participatory approaches strategic design solutions for these places. Also playing a role are the cultural landscape of the Cañada Real Galiana in the case of Madrid, as well as a comprehension of natural hazards in the case of Canaan. In these projects, collaboration with ethnologists, geologists, and hydrologists is central to the approach.

The projects in Jakarta and Bali pursue the notion of analytical research trips dedicated to examining and decoding interdependencies between waves of new urbanization and the traditional landscape. They are understood as a first step towards developing a long-term solution to problems—since, in these places, shortsighted and short-winded design fantasies have proved to be absurd.

What all ten projects share is the fact that they consist of explorations and do not claim any finality. In the complex and unpredictable situations relating to the rapid urbanization of very diverse cultural circles and geographies, there can be no panaceas or best practices. As the anthropogeographer Frauke Kraas has stipulated in her lectures, only an in-depth and broad understanding of context can lead to site- and culture-specific possibilities for development. As representatives of a "dirty" discipline that counters what Bruno Latour identifies as the separation between the natural, social, and engineering sciences, with the practice of transforming space, we hope that the contents and working methods of our projects will contribute to producing knowledge that makes it possible to overcome the narrow boundaries of the disciplines and with them, the traditional binaries of city and landscape, culture and nature, and as such will be able to facilitate comprehensive and holistic approaches.

●

John Beardsley

In from the Margins:
Landscape Architecture and
Extreme Urbanism

By now, it is widely acknowledged in the design and planning worlds that we live in an urban age, with over half the world's population inhabiting cities—a percentage that is sure to grow. It is also broadly recognized that a significant percentage of city dwellers around the world—perhaps as much as a third—lives in substandard conditions. Recent United Nations estimates suggest that nearly a billion people, primarily in the developing countries of the Global South, live in circumstances that fit the classic definition of slums, characterized by overcrowding, precarious housing, inadequate access to clean water and sanitation, and insecure land tenure. Many live in informal settlements known variously as squatter communities or shantytowns, often in extreme environmental conditions— steep slopes, floodplains, or contaminated sites—and isolated from employment and transportation infrastructure. But the problems of uneven development extend beyond such marginal communities. Formal planning and design processes are often unable to keep pace with the demand for urban development, especially in larger cities in the developing world, with profound environmental consequences. Increased storm water runoff from developed lands, for instance, typically leads to increased urban flooding and landslides. Add to this the impact of natural forces intensified by climate change, whether hurricanes and typhoons or rising sea levels, and the environmental conditions of urban areas, particularly along the coasts, seem almost unimaginably complex.

In recent years, planning and development agencies, non-governmental organizations, and designers have all turned their attention to the emerging problems of urban landscapes, with some notable successes. Medellín, Columbia, and São Paulo, Brazil, have both won accolades for their efforts to improve living conditions for their lower-income residents through initiatives to connect informal or extra-legal settlements to water, sanitary, and transportation infrastructures. These projects exemplify the fact that prevailing strategies among municipal officials, planners, and designers for addressing such "informal" settlements have shifted away from the kinds of large-scale slum clearance and relocations typical of the modernist era, which were demonstrated to cause massive social disruptions, toward on-site upgrading and improvement, with the goal of integrating these low-income communities into their larger urban contexts.

But the scale of urban environmental problems continues to outpace the solutions available through municipal budgets and conventional planning and design strategies. In response, both design professionals and academic researchers have turned their individual energies to analyzing urban landscape conditions and formulating strategies to address them. Urban Think Tank, a design practice established in Caracas in 1998, and Estudio Teddy Cruz, an experimental practice in social and spatial research based in San Diego, are examples from the Americas of something increasingly common around the world: practitioners who are taking it upon themselves to address the problems of advancing urbanization through social entrepreneurship or, more rarely, through the creation of not-for-profit research arms of for-profit design practices.

But it is increasingly in the academic context that the complex conditions of urban social conflict, environmental degradation, and risks of climate change are being investigated. Such is the case with the work documented in this publication. It presents projects by five design-research teams led principally by German academics based in universities in Germany and Australia, but examining the challenges of extreme landscapes in cities around the globe, including Madrid, Casablanca, Kigali, Port-au-Prince, Medellín, Lima, São Paulo,

Changde, and Jakarta. What is notable about this group is that they all come from the discipline of landscape architecture. Nine years ago, when Christian Werthmann, one of the designers represented here, and I organized *Dirty Work,* an exhibition for the Harvard Graduate School of Design on efforts to upgrade environmental conditions in low-income urban communities in Latin America, all our case studies came from either architecture or from urban planning and design—not from landscape architecture. Now, the issues of environmental justice and social inequality in the world's developing cities have moved toward the center of landscape design practice, especially in the context of academic research.

Looking across the range of this work, a few generalities can be affirmed. Perhaps not surprisingly, these landscape professionals all recognize the landscape as something with both physical and cultural dimensions, a mosaic of different uses that are intertwined, complex, and often fragmented. All take a landscape-scale approach to the problems of the city. Storm water management, sewage and garbage disposal, ground subsidence, landslides, and food production and security are not isolated challenges, but interconnected phenomena that need to be addressed at the scale of the city. These challenges often require an ad hoc, incremental approach, however, and a commitment to experimental solutions that, if they work, might be extrapolated to a systems-wide scale. New paradigms of design research and practice are also in evidence here: The magnitude of environmental challenges in the city requires greater collaboration and more interdisciplinary approaches. The research presented here is as much social, even ethnographic, as it is environmental or historical. While a few of these projects question or even push back against entrenched urban actors, every one of them reveals the wide range of players and competing interests in the contemporary city. Most of the designers are quite explicit about the efforts they make to engage the subjects of their studies, facilitating their participation in design research and development in an effort to avoid top-down proposals. In several instances, as in the case of Medellín, proposed scenarios are based on shared understandings of benefits rather than on prohibitions against particular actions or uses. Overall, the projects documented here suggest that an inventive process, especially one that recognizes and develops local narratives through community participation, can facilitate or even inspire design outcomes.

Perhaps most heartening from the perspective of the landscape historian, the sites under scrutiny here are not presented as if they have no history: they are presented within the context of sophisticated contextual research. What is described as "the biggest slum in Europe," for instance, takes an attenuated linear shape outside of Madrid because it occupies an ancient, royally decreed right-of-way for sheep drovers. The rice paddies of Bali, increasingly overwhelmed by untreated sewage outflow from residential development, are understood as an expression of a centuries-old, cooperative, socio-religious system of water management. In the same way, Changde is presented as "a dry city in a wet landscape" that once functioned as part of a hydraulic system that has now been largely erased.

Equally heartening is the sense of commitment that comes across in these projects to addressing what can seem like overwhelming problems. Still more, this commitment is conveyed with some measure of optimism, and a sense that landscape solutions can provide social as well as environmental benefits. In the proposal for Casablanca, for instance, agriculture is embraced not only for its role in food production and security, but also for its climate-moderating effects and for educational and employment opportunities. In the case of Jakarta, we are asked to rethink our assumptions: to think of flooding not as a disaster but as the expression of seasonally recurring events; to think of disasters as opportunities to demonstrate resilience in our thinking and our actions. We have cause to be wary of optimism as it is applied to some of the challenges examined here: informal urbanism, whether in Kigali or Lima, is arguably one of the most consequential and potentially disruptive sites of social conflict and spatial inequality in the twenty-first century. Yet even here, there are things we can do: slope stabilization, reforestation, sewage treatment wetlands, and water harvesting in addition to improved infrastructure—if we can muster either the political will or the economic resources to do so.

It has been nearly fifty years since Ian McHarg published his celebrated book, *Design with Nature,* which signaled as much as anything the coming of age of the environmental design movement. McHarg described his book as an "ecological manual for the good steward who aspires to art." In hindsight, he looks more like a planner than a designer, an analyst who imagined alternative scenarios for landscape transformation rather than a steward who aspired to art. It has been left to subsequent generations of landscape architects to flesh out his manual, combining ecological awareness with environmentalist agendas and design aspirations. It is the fruits of just such efforts that are presented here.

Jürgen Renn

On the Construction Sites of the Anthropocene

Humankind has changed the planet Earth to a degree comparable to geological forces. There is barely any natural environment left. The history of humankind has become inscribed in the history of the Earth. Scientists are discussing the idea of linking this upheaval to a new geological era, the Anthropocene, which has already left behind deep traces on our planet. The Earth system as a whole is changing in a way for which there are hardly any analogies in the history of the Earth.

This is the global perspective that has resulted from scientific investigations in recent decades, which have incorporated numerous research activities so as to provide an in-depth analysis of the Earth system. The works presented in this catalogue take a different perspective. They were engendered by encounters with the concrete challenges posed at hotspots of this transformation process: rapidly expanding megacities where people attempt to lead dignified lives under precarious conditions. If, however, one wanted to use these projects just to illustrate the larger context of the Anthropocene, this would fall short in a decisive respect.

In the age of the Anthropocene, the possibilities of steering global processes by human action are controversially discussed. Some propose global interventions, in the sense of geo-engineering, global governance, or a change in the global economic order. Many point to the futility of such interventions, while others see the further journey into the Anthropocene as being predefined by systemic constraints. In contrast, the projects presented here reveal realistic opportunities for action that pertain to the local as well as the global dimensions of the Anthropocene. Against this backdrop, they represent a significant contribution to the discourse on the Anthropocene.

The conditions in which humankind lives are more precarious than assumed. Nature is not a stable stage on which the life of human beings plays out; it participates in the drama. Nature is also not an independent variable, but instead part of a complex system that is also shaped by human societies. The traditional reference system, in which nature and culture are separate, no longer fits. Human history has become the history of nature in a twofold sense: it has planetary effects, and it follows a logic in which this situation cannot be understood from the perspective of an autonomy of human actions.

These two aspects seem to imply a causal connection, which is, however, a contentious question. On the one hand, the claim has been made that the human effects on the history of nature are only possible because human actions are not autonomous, but instead already part of a natural history of things. Or the reverse claim is made that human actions have such a fatal effect on the Earth system because they have not yet sufficiently freed themselves from this dependence on natural history. In this confrontation, an age-old dualism has assumed a new guise: the attempt to establish a complicity with the forces of destiny—if necessary also at the price of surrendering human subjectivity or other forms of self-sacrifice—is juxtaposed with the attempt to achieve human autonomy by definitely subordinating the planet under the superior power of human ingenuity.

In the language of the Anthropocene, this is the contrast between a technosphere that is becoming increasingly independent of human action, including all technical systems and infrastructures and the people involved in them, and an anthroposphere that is not yet sufficiently emancipated from technical, economic, or political constraints. In both cases, we are not primarily concerned with utopian visions but rather with an understanding of the global processes in which humankind is involved.

While the concept of an "anthroposphere" is used here to summarily describe the complex social processes in the Anthropocene, the geophysicist Peter Haff has established rules for the concept of the technosphere that specify the relation between human activities and the global system into which they are integrated. The first, "the rule of inaccessibility," states that the technosphere is not able to directly influence the behavior of its human "components." It instead follows its own logic, without any consideration of its components—just as computer users do not directly influence the individual components of their computers. The second rule, "the rule of impotence," in contrast, refers to the fact that most individuals are unable to influence the behavior of large technical systems. The third rule, "the rule of control," concerns people's difficulty in controlling technical systems with a larger range of behaviors than they themselves have. The fourth rule, "the rule of reciprocity," moreover states that people can only enter into effective interaction with systems of their own order of magnitude. The fifth rule, "the rule of performance," describes how people are pressured to perpetuate the technosphere, while the sixth rule, "the rule of provision," in contrast, notes that the technosphere, for its part, has to guarantee that people function as components of the system. If this analysis applies to the present or the near future, there are few possibilities of escaping this logic in which human beings increasingly become subordinate elements in a global process of transformation.

The projects and experiences presented here speak a different language. Although traces of the Anthropocene can clearly be found in all of them, they simultaneously testify to possibilities of resisting this logic and of shaping processes of transformation. As Karl Marx suggested, human beings continue to write their own history, albeit not voluntarily or under conditions that they themselves choose. This insight, however, takes on a new relevance under the conditions of the Anthropocene, since, given the existence of planetary limits, the scope for action is shrinking more and more. Both aspects—the limited formability and finiteness of our world—can be conceived within the concept of the "ergosphere": the sphere of human work and creations, with all their ambivalence, for which rules can also be framed.

In contrast to the technosphere, what applies to the ergosphere is "the rule of accessibility," our first rule. In contrast to the circuits of a computer, we human beings are, in principle, in a position to understand the superordinate logic in which we are involved as a result of the dynamics of the Earth system. The entirety of this change is reflected—of course via manifold mediations—in human knowledge, which simultaneously represents a potential for global action.

The second rule, "the rule of empowerment," states that we can also utilize this knowledge in seemingly hopeless situations so as to shape changes. As a result of climate change and increasing urbanization, an increasing number of people are being exposed to the risk of landslides. "Modernization" measures that dictate from above a certain rationale to local conditions prove to be contra-productive. As the example of the informal settlements on the hillsides of Medellín shows, it is possible to cope with any risks involved if those who are immediately affected are put in a position to link knowledge pertaining to them with their own interests, experiences, and local possibilities for action. The result is not a universal solution but rather a differentiated combination of global and local knowledge.

The third rule, the "rule of exploration and adaptation," states that the problem does not consist of human beings not being able to control systems that have a larger range of behaviors than they do themselves, but rather in what "control"

might mean in the first place. Our third rule suggests that the stewardship of technological systems and infrastructures depends on their specific nature, in particular their embedding in natural and cultural environments, as well as on their representation by knowledge and belief systems. If people succeed in sufficiently discerning the environmental system of which they are part by exploring its potentials and adapting flexibly to it, they at least have the chance to survive in it, even if the system itself is subject to rapid changes. As the example of Jakarta shows, this is first and foremost a question of realistically assessing local possibilities for action, which are increasingly defined by global climate change and the unfettered growth of this city and its gradual sinking into the water. In the case of the new city of Canaan, with its inhospitable living conditions and unplanned spread to the north of Port-au-Prince, cooperatively developing and sharing knowledge, as well as recognizing local possibilities for adaptation have also proven to be crucial preconditions for being in the position to deal with looming natural catastrophes such as flooding.

The fourth rule, "the rule of couplings and interfaces," focuses on the nonlinear interdependencies between the ergosphere and the other spheres of the Earth that are connected by metabolic and other cycles. As a result of these couplings, human action can potentially result in catastrophic instabilities in the Earth system. Then again, by creating suitable interfaces, human beings can also stabilize such cycles, as the example of a project for Grand Casablanca shows: it envisages a spatial interleaving of urban and agricultural structures, which would not only have a favorable influence on the climate, but also contribute to the provisioning of urban residents. This rule emphasizes the critical role of the particularities of local circumstances, as is shown by the example of the wetlands of Rwanda's capital Kigali, which offers a similar opportunity for novel couplings between material flows and improved resource management through the integration of agricultural use in the city.

The fifth rule, "the rule of repurposing," points to another distinctive feature of the ergosphere, the fact that the means that people employ can also be utilized beyond their original purposes. This insight is a double-edged sword: on the one hand, it limits the compulsive character of technology and offers opportunities to innovate; on the other, it requires that responsibility for the use of technical systems always be assumed anew. Two examples in this book substantiate this ambivalence. In Bali, a sophisticated, communally operated irrigation system has supplied the rice field terraces with water since ancient times. The island now has 4.3 million inhabitants and is visited, in addition, by some eight million tourists each year. This has resulted in the traditional irrigation system increasingly being repurposed as a sewer. The acute water supply problems of the Peruvian capital, Lima, in contrast, could possibly be resolved, in part, by repurposing the existing sewers so that instead of flowing directly into the sea or into rivers, they supply recreational parks, which in turn could contribute to the purification of wastewater. Similar considerations are behind the idea of "sponge cities" in China.

The sixth and final rule, "the rule of exposure," states that the ergosphere, in contrast to the technosphere, does not imply any guaranteed supply for its human actors. It is, therefore, in no way possible for us to assume that the technical systems we have constructed will also ensure our survival in future if we are not prepared to continually adapt them. A starting point is provided by insights into the unintended consequences of our actions, which we must disclose if they are to have any feedback effects on our thinking and actions. One example of this is the proposal to once again provide access to the Tamanduateí River, which was encased in concrete in the course of industrialization and currently flows, malodorous and inaccessible, as the liquid middle strip of an expressway in São Paulo. By exposing this situation, the lack of recreation areas in a megacity would turn into a publically visible problem.

In all of the projects addressed here, extensive historical experience also plays a role, whether the hydraulic legacy of China or ancient livestock routes in Spain, a legacy that offers creative potential also for the discourse on current challenges. This also differentiates the ergosphere from the technosphere: it does not present us with the false alternative of either surrendering ourselves to the internal dynamics of global technological systems or having to plan them from scratch. Rather, it invites us to see ourselves as part of a co-evolutionary process in which our possibilities for action also depend on the knowledge that we are able to obtain about this process.

Undine Giseke,
Kathrin Wieck,
Christoph Kasper

Casablanca

1

Casablanca, Morocco
             Fields—the Hidden Face of the City

             When you drive from the port of Casablanca along
the coast toward the southwest, after twenty-five kilometers, you reach
Dar Bouazza, a small coastal city on the Atlantic that is a popular destination for bathing excursions. On the way there, you pass the newly
constructed marina, the Grand Mosque, the site with the lighthouse and
the fancy restaurants, the Corniche, the huge Morocco Mall. At some
point, the city of white buildings, with its compact urban corpus, ends
abruptly and fields spread out, running downhill to the Atlantic as long,
narrow plots of land. But the break only lasts a short time. The road
soon continues through four- and five-story new housing estates, alter-
nating with dense, informal settlements, interrupted anew by linear field
structures, this time parallel to the coastline. When you approach Dar
Bouazza, the picture changes once again. Here, splinters of informal
settlements, business clusters, luxurious single-family houses, and fields
give rise to a small-scale patchwork. You also see similar sequences of
spaces when you leave Grand Casablanca, the urban region, on traffic
arteries to the south and east. But here you soon encounter other urban
cores such as Tit Mellil, Bouskoura, Mediouna, the airport city, or the
neighboring coastal city of Mohammedia.
             What rules does the development of such spatial
structures follow? What aspects are the result of planning, and what, in
contrast, results from uncontrolled processes? Which structures can be
regarded as a transitional stage, which represent a permanent pheno-
menon, and how will they develop further? Within the framework of the
Bundesministerium für Bildung und Forschung's (BMBF: Federal Ministry
of Education and Research) Future Megacities research program, a
nine-year research project (2005–14) dealt with these questions, at first
analytically, and then through doing conceptual and concrete testing
(Giseke et al. 2015).

◀   Connecting spheres—the urban and the rural, 2015

▲ Ouled Ahmed: The overlapping of urban and rural practices
in everyday life, 2015

The basic frameworks of urban development, agriculture, the climate situation, the provision of infrastructure, and the conditions of governance were recorded on site. As part of this, a retrospective analysis showed that the urbanization of Casablanca in recent years has tended toward a polycentric and fragmented development of the urban region, resulting in diverse interlinkages of urban and rural structures. This is often only regarded as a transitional state that will be overcome by further urbanization. Various analyses, scenarios, and modeling approaches nonetheless made it clear that the development of a coherent structure of the built environment within the urban region as a whole cannot be expected, despite further urbanization. Grand Casablanca is growing rapidly. In 2004, 3.63 million inhabitants lived on 23,600 hectares of urbanized area; one year later, there were 4.27 million. The population is expected to exceed five million by 2030 at the latest. By then—according to the master plan for urban development of 2008— another 23,000-hectare area of the urban region, with its total of 120,000 hectares, will have been built up. But, even then, there will still be more then 55,000 hectares of agricultural land remaining in the urban region (AUC 2008). It is, however, not the absolute figures that are important, but rather orders of magnitude. Agriculture, for which there is no adequate development concept, will remain a giant in land use in the urban region for the foreseeable future. In contrast to other megacities, Grand Casablanca does have a planning system on multiple levels and the current land-use plan does address the preservation of agricultural areas for the first time, but dealing with its fields has not been operationalized accordingly. Plans, programs, and political guidelines between city and agriculture do not correspond. There are also no concepts for open-space planning. All of this results in incoherent urban development that deviates from (integrated) planning and does not recognize the value for the city of landscape and agricultural areas. The land use giant agriculture remains a dwarf with respect to its function and possible effect on the urban region.

It is with this problem that the research project started. The aspects examined were what role agriculture might play in the future urban region and whether it might be possible to develop closer interaction between urban and rural structures.

Challenging current urbanization three central topic fields have emerged. First, as a result of its morphological links to various scale levels, agriculture can contribute to climate-optimized urban development as the complementary green space in the urban region. This was made clear by the analyses and modeling done by climate experts. Grand Casablanca is characterized by an arid, subtropic climate. While the city's historical orientation toward the sea benefits from cooling by Atlantic winds, despite high (structural) density, the ever-further expanding hot, dry hinterland is threatened by the risk of extreme heat island formation. A spatial interlinkage of urban and rural structures would increase the surface roughness and could stimulate cooling internal circulation.

Second, in the urban development up to now, another aspect has also received too little attention: integrated urban agriculture can contribute significantly to the urban food supply. For a long time, nutrition was marked out as a need for which the city was responsible and a blind spot in planning. The reason for this lies in the historically developed dualism of

▲ City and agriculture in the urbanizing region of Grand Casablanca, 2015

▲ Rapid growth and density in the historical center of Casablanca, 2015

▲ Decoupled urban-rural land use structures in Grand Casablanca, 2010

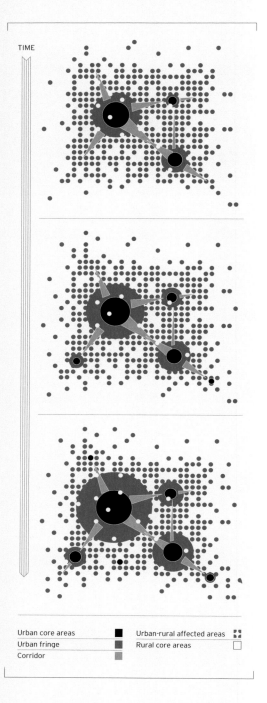

TIME

Urban core areas	■	Urban-rural affected areas	⚏
Urban fringe	■	Rural core areas	☐
Corridor	■		

The permanence of the linkages between urban and rural spheres in polycentric urban regions

city and countryside and the decoupling of food production, which was (and still is) assigned to rural areas and the agrarian economy, and the city as a place of private food consumption. The demands to feed growing urban systems around the globe are huge. Their great vulnerability in the case of ever-increasing dependency on the global agricultural market leads to a need to put a greater focus on the competence of cities and urban regions in matters of food production. How can agriculture integrated into urban areas become a supporting pillar in an urban-regional food system and make a contribution to the food security and food sovereignty of the urban region? Our scenarios show that increasing the share of irrigation farming would be able to supply up to fifty percent of the urban region's demand for fruit and vegetables.

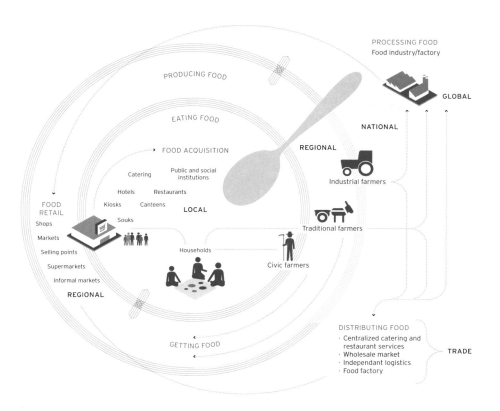

PROCESSING FOOD
Food industry/factory

GLOBAL

PRODUCING FOOD

NATIONAL

EATING FOOD

REGIONAL

FOOD ACQUISITION

Catering   Public and social
            institutions

Hotels   Restaurants

Kiosks   Canteens   LOCAL

Industrial farmers

Souks

FOOD
RETAIL

Shops

Markets

Selling points

Supermarkets

Informal markets

REGIONAL

Households

Traditional farmers

Civic farmers

DISTRIBUTING FOOD
· Centralized catering and
  restaurant services
· Wholesale market
· Independant logistics
· Food factory

TRADE

GETTING FOOD

▲ Social, economic, and spatial linkages of the urban food
   system

Third, and finally, if we think of city and agriculture as interacting systems, what options for the organization and linking of metabolic cycles result from this? How can different flows of materials in the urban region—food, water, energy, waste— be coupled with one another and organized in an integrated way? In the concrete case of Grand Casablanca, there was a specific time window for linking the urban and rural water regimes, since the entire infrastructure for water disposal and treatment was first and still is in the process of being developed. After many years of diverting wastewater into the Atlantic, for the most part unpurified, the first wastewater treatment plants have been built in the last few years. They offer the possibility to utilize purified city water in agriculture and to increase the percentage of irrigation farming using a systematic approach. Agriculture will thus also become more attractive economically for the many small farmers of the region.

The possible development of various urban-rural morphologies in the entire urban region

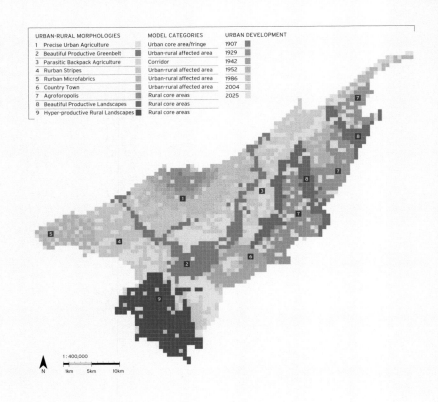

URBAN-RURAL MORPHOLOGIES	MODEL CATEGORIES	URBAN DEVELOPMENT
1 Precise Urban Agriculture	Urban core area/fringe	1907
2 Beautiful Productive Greenbelt	Urban-rural affected area	1929
3 Parasitic Backpack Agriculture	Corridor	1942
4 Rurban Stripes	Urban-rural affected area	1952
5 Rurban Microfabrics	Urban-rural affected area	1986
6 Country Town	Urban-rural affected area	2004
7 Agroforopolis	Rural core areas	2025
8 Beautiful Productive Landscapes	Rural core areas	
9 Hyper-productive Rural Landscapes	Rural core areas	

1 : 400,000

N   1km   5km   10km

There were various obstacles to overcome in such a broad, interdisciplinary research structure. In the first instance, this comprised the fact that there are no theoretical foundations and urbanistic concepts for bringing together urban and rural spheres of an urban region that are tailored to the current conditions in the urban growth centers of the Global South. Many existing models are oriented toward individual functions or monocentric structures. Urban concepts that take into account and spatialize flows and processes of exchange only partially exist. Classic urban planning concepts such as the garden city model of Ebenezer Howard, the Broadacre City of Frank Lloyd Wright, or the Agricultural City of Kisho Kurokawa are normative concepts for a conceived space. They are no longer suitable for providing appropriate answers to the generative processes of spatial production, the constraints of planning practice, the integration of top-down and bottom-up activities, and hence the wide range of actors and varying interests in processes of urbanization today.

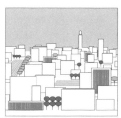
1 Precise Urban Agriculture

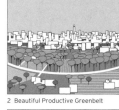
2 Beautiful Productive Greenbelt

3 Parasitic Backpack Agriculture

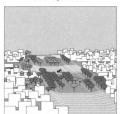
4 Rurban stripes

5 Rurban Microfabrics

6 Country Town

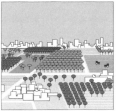
7 Agroforopolis

8 Beautiful Productive Landscapes

9 Hyper-productive Rural Landscapes

► Nine urban-rural morphologies as categories of spatial system linkages

URBAN SPHERE   RURAL SPHERE

In order to bring spheres that have up to now been regarded as separate and incompatible into interaction, it was necessary for all the individuals involved to leave behind old categorical attributions of city and countryside, since this was the only way for alternative development options to become conceivable. The basis for the initiation of such multilayered processes was the creation of aims and visions in common ownership beyond disciplinary borders, something that took place in various formats such as planning workshops or in the collaborative development of scenarios. As a result of these processes, what was generated was a multidimensional strategy with various conceptual building blocks in which diverse spatial and functional links as well as new socioeconomic collaborations between the two spheres were shown. Agriculture therefore becomes the coproducer of the urban, and the city also the coproducer of the rural. The approach aims at a partial re-territorializing of processes of exchange on the scale of the urban region. Agriculture becomes a productive green infrastructure for the urban region, from which the city benefits. At the same time, agriculture benefits from nearby markets with their huge demand for agricultural products and from an ongoing provision of urban resources such as purified city water or organic waste.

The concept for strengthening these levels of cooperation was developed as an "incrementalist" approach that—adhering to a pragmatic urbanism—offers a wide range of parallel courses of action. In the central spatial-morphological building block, the urban region is conceived as a permeable overlay of urban and rural structures, naturally with very different physical manifestations in terms of granularity and density, depending on the respective starting situation. The different urban-rural morphologies range from agricultural micro-area, such as rooftop terraces and community gardens in dense urban districts, to productive parks in the form of greenbelts or green bands that structure the city and its districts. In other areas of the urban region, the relationship is reversed. Here, agriculture forms the basis for the integration of individual urban islands of use and infrastructures. Nonetheless, in future, agriculture will develop here in a clearly multifunctional way, including recreational opportunities for city dwellers, as a result of walking paths and picnic areas for example. These morphological categories form the basis for an urban structure characterized by productive green space.

Research was also done by means of design work. Urban design and landscape-architectural design was used as a method to materialize and organize knowledge in order to spatialize and implement this new topic-specific knowledge. Accompanying the research, design solutions were developed in university design studios, international summer schools, or as student degree theses, but also as an immanent part of the research in an urban design competition or in transdisciplinary workshops organized by the research project. We practiced systemic design for linking the urban and the rural. The results led the various research participants away from status-quo thinking and toward a process of imagining how the nearly intractable "wicked problems" (Brown et al. 2010) might be approached by means of a concrete change in spatial practice.

Work was done—under the coordination of a landscape architect—in a large interdisciplinary team with experts from various specialist disciplines such as urban planners and urban economists, climate researchers, water specialists, agrarian and social scientists, each in German-Moroccan research tandems. The team, which included up to sixty individuals in some phases, also involved representatives from practice and comprised actors from the municipal and regional administration, from non-governmental organizations, associations, businesses, and schools as well as farmers and community initiatives. It therefore adhered to the new research principle of transdisciplinary research, with its focus on generating problem-solving knowledge for concrete social transformations. Such a research approach produces not only systems knowledge—thus in-depth knowledge about various facets of a problem—but also target and transformation knowledge with a view to stimulating concrete changes in society.

Four pilot projects established specific spaces to test how new links might be created on various levels of scale and action, each with different thematic focuses, by means of metabolic material flows or socioeconomic components. They served as concrete synergy generators at specifically targeted locations in the urban region. In the first pilot project, possible synergies between the sectors of agriculture and industry were addressed with a view to extensive reutilization of purified city water in agriculture. Within the framework of the second pilot project, it was possible to realize the construction of a community garden on an area for interim use in the informal settlement of Ouled Ahmed. Here it was shown how the purified wastewater of a neighboring hammam can be used for irrigation. In the community garden, women were, moreover, also taught ecological farming methods. With the third project, possible links between agriculture near the city and touristic activities were tried and tested in a valley with exceptionally attractive scenery in order to ensure the preservation of agriculture and hence the cultural landscape through a diversification of revenues. The fourth pilot project, in Dar Bouazza, demonstrated how it is possible with the production of agricultural products to train small farmers in agroecological farming methods and to market organic food baskets as an attractive business model in a new producer-consumer network.

The pilot project in Dar Bouazza: ensuring agricultural use through the development of a producer-consumer network ▼

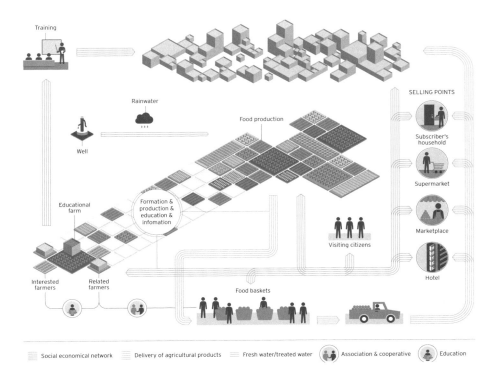

Training

Rainwater

Food production

Well

SELLING POINTS

Subscriber's household

Supermarket

Educational farm

Formation & production & education & infomation

Marketplace

Visiting citizens

Hotel

Interested farmers

Related farmers

Food baskets

≡ Social economical network   ≡ Delivery of agricultural products   ≡ Fresh water/treated water   👥 Association & cooperative   👤 Education

▲ Packing the organic baskets for distribution at the
pedagogical farm, 2011

▼ The pilot project of the pedagogical farm: regional food
production as part of the green infrastructure of the urban
region, 2010

All the pilot projects were developed and anchored in close cooperation with civil-society actors. The social spectrum of the actors was broad and ranged, depending on the topic, from various farmers to industrial businesses and wastewater treatment plant operators to street venders and residents of informal settlements. The four pilot projects were not only concrete implementation locations, but serve as learning platforms explicitly for exchange between civil-society actors, scientists, and municipal experts. Future workshops, exhibitions, action days as well as films and media appearances were further formats that also allowed the broader public, in addition to the research team, to take part in the research process and the questions discussed within it. Through summer schools, design studios, and master's theses, research was intensively linked to teaching.

The project approach toward an altered urban-rural order and linking it on economic, socio-cultural, and spatial levels shakes up existing systems and softens previous boundaries. Paradoxically, through doing so, the project initially gave rise to a problem that had not previously existed at all in the perception of the urban region. From the integrated viewpoint initiated arose a new hypercomplexity, which characterizes many processes in the Anthropocene, but also generates resistance. As a result of the inter- and transdisciplinary working method over many years within the framework of the project, it was nonetheless possible to make visible the qualities for an altered coexistence leading to stable and resilient development of the region. All the participants therefore had to readjust their positioning with respect to the landscape and the city again and again. The Western myth of the beautiful landscape of Petrarca as an ideal image consequently faded further, but—to paraphrase Humphrey Bogart's legendary closing words in the classic film *Casablanca*—it might be the beginning of a beautiful friendship between the two spheres.

•

Project data

Project title
Urban Agriculture as an Integrative Factor of Climate-Optimized Urban Development in Casablanca, Morocco

German-Moroccan research project in the framework of the Future Megacities Research Program of the German Federal Ministry of Education and Research (BMBF)

Project management
TU Berlin, Department of Landscape Architecture + Open Space Planning, coordinated by Prof. Undine Giseke

Staff members
Juliane Brandt (2012–14), Georg Bock (2013), Anne-Katrin Fenk (2009), Silvia Martin Han (2007–12), David Kaufmann (2013), Christoph Kasper (2010–14), Yassine Moustanjidi (2012–14), Chloé Naneix (2011–13), Meggi Pieschel (2008–11), Kathrin Wieck (2005, 2011–14)

German project partners
TU Berlin, Department of Climatology, Prof. Dr. Dieter Scherer; TU Berlin, Department of Process Engineering, Prof. Dr. Matthias Kraume (coordination of pilot project 1); TU Berlin, ZEWK kubus, Gisela Prystav, Dr. Frank Helten (coordination of pilot project 2); University of Hohenheim: Department for Agricultural Communication and Extension, Dr. Maria Gerster-Bentaya (coordination of pilot project 2); Bergische Universität Wuppertal: Department of Economics of Planning and Construction, Prof. Dr. Guido Spars; fbr e. V. Darmstadt: Fachvereinigung Betriebs- und Regenwassernutzung e. V., Dietmar Sperfeld

Moroccan project partners
National Institute of Spatial Planning and Urbanism Rabat (INAU); Casablanca University Hassan II, Ain Chock, School of Science, Chair of Hydroscience and Mohammedia, School of Sciences Ben M'Sik; City Planning Authority for Casablanca Region (AUC); Regional Authority of Agriculture in Casablanca Region (DRA); Regional Authority of Housing, Urbanism and Spatial Planning, Casablanca (IRHUAE); National Weather Service, Casablanca (DMN); Association Terre et Humanisme Maroc, Casablanca (T&H); Association Unions of Ouled Ahmed and School of Ouled Ahmed, Douar Hmar

Duration
preliminary phase 2005–08; main phase 2008–14

▼ Transdisciplinary research and knowledge integration: scenario workshop in Casablanca in 2010

Azzedine Hafif, Abdelkader Kaioua, Mohammed El Haddi

Stimulating Change in Institutional Practices

"Today, Urban Agriculture is considered by many experts and professional urban planners more than a simple economic activity to promote harmonious and sustainable development of a city, but a real ideological trend in favor of a model for an alternative urban development that aims to balance economic performance, social equity, and the preservation of natural resources. In Morocco, the concerns of sustainable urban development emerged in the early 2000s during the organization of the Débat National sur Aménagement du Territoire (National Debate on Regional Planning). Since 2005, the AUC has been one of the most active partners of the UAC project, having acknowledged the Urban Agriculture concept as innovative and a carrier of a new philosophy of sustainable urban development. We must admit that Urban Agriculture has never been protected under the former urban planning documents that have governed Casablanca town planning. The farming land located within the urban perimeter has rather been perceived as a mere land reserve awaiting urbanization. Urban planning's main concern has always been to respond to pressing housing, social and public needs amidst the rapid pace of urbanization that has prevailed in this city" (Hafif in Adidi et al 2015, p. 454).

"Now, at the time of the establishment of a new urban policy that would break with the sectoral and technicist approaches that have prevailed so far in urban planning, urban policy is intended as a participatory and bottom-up approach based on integration, universality, sustainability and good governance. It is against the background of this new framework that Urban Agriculture can become a lever for social and sustainable urban development. Since the inception of the UAC project, the IRHUPV as a stakeholder in this project has appropriated and engaged in the dissemination of the Urban Agriculture concept.

In all the scientific and political events organized in Grand Casablanca in which the Inspection was a participant, information and sensitization campaigns pertaining to the Urban Agriculture concept were conducted, targeting elected representatives and urban planning decision makers, notably at the AUC" (Kaioua in Adidi et al 2015, p. 454).

"[Also] the Grand Casablanca DRA was among the first institutions to have supported the UAC project. The concept of Urban Agriculture has been promoted by the DRA based on the idea that Casablanca is not only an industrial and tertiary metropolis, but also an agricultural one" (El Haddi in Adidi et al 2015, p. 455).

"The new Grand Casablanca Master Plan approved in 2010 aims to break with the urban planning approaches and methods that have prevailed in Casablanca since the colonial period. This new document aims to be global, integrated and participatory. One of the innovations contained in this master plan is the promotion of green spaces as structural components of urban development. Urban Agriculture is, of course, not yet recognized as an urban economic function, but it is now beginning to enjoy some kind of protection through regulations, notably in rural communities such as Mediouna, Nouaceur, and Echellalat. Besides the new areas that will be included in Casablancas urban perimeter, the new master plan prioritizes harmonious development of the city" (Hafif in Adidi et al 2015, p. 454).

"The next steps will be crucial, as its objective is to advocate for the institutionalization and acknowledgement of Urban Agriculture in Grand Casablanca, strengthening the already existing unit and sensitizing actors and local peri-urban authorities to the need to preserve Urban Agriculture on their land" (Kaioua in Adidi et al 2015, p. 455).

Undine Giseke,
Juliane Brandt,
Christoph Kasper

Kigali

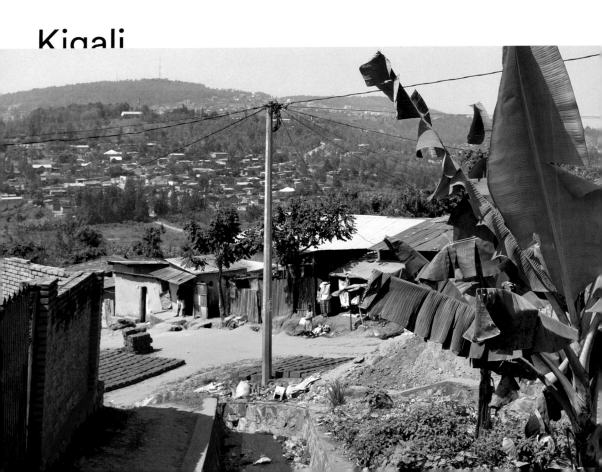

2

Kigali, Rwanda
City of Hills and Wetlands

Kigali, the still young capital of Rwanda, bears the name of a mountain. How did this come about? The emergence of the city is closely linked to the Berlin Conference, which took place in Berlin in 1884–85 and sought to regulate European trade and colonization of Africa. Germany subsequently took over the administration of parts of East Africa, including what is today the national territory of Rwanda, and retained it until the end of World War I. In 1907, Richard Kandt, a physician and Africa explorer, was commissioned to set up a Residentur (an administrative outpost) in Rwanda and as the site for this selected the stretch of land called Nyarugenge, which is located in the center of the country, opposite Mount Kigali. The complex, local name did not prevail, and the location was henceforth named after the mountain.

◀ Connecting systems – hills and wetlands, 2016

Rapid growth:
expansion of the
settlement area within
one century

Kigali and other military outposts formed the first urbanized centers in the up to that time rural country that was characterized by dispersed settlements. In 1907 there were 357 individuals in Kigali, predominantly traders. Until independence in 1962, the process of urbanization proceeded extremely slowly. The rural space was clearly given precedence by the colonial powers— as of 1918, Rwanda was a territory under Belgian mandate. Rwandans were prohibited from moving to the city without proof of employment. When the country gained independence in 1962 it had the lowest degree of urbanization in the world, with only 2.4% (Manirakiza 2011, pp. 4–6). Kigali was a small city with 6,000 inhabitants. As the new capital, it became a focus for migration by the rural population. In 1991, shortly before the genocide, it had 235,664 inhabitants. The young republic was only able to deal with growth requirements in an unsatisfactory manner. Although there were master plans in the 1960s and 1980s, they did not become the basis for the growth of the city.

An enormous drop in population figures occurred in the 1990s due to the civil war and the genocide, in 1994, which led to a wave of outward migration. It is estimated that the population in 1994 was only 50,000 inhabitants (Manirakiza 2011, p. 9). After the war, growth accelerated as a result of migrants returning from neighboring countries and newcomers from the provinces, who perceived the city as a protective space. Between 2003 and 2013, the population more than doubled: to 1.3 million inhabitants today. The influx continues, exceeding previous growth forecasts. To meet the huge demand for housing, the city has expanded tremendously. A large number of unplanned settlements lacking in infrastructure facilities have come into being. They constitute seventy to eighty percent of the existing settlements and are often located on slopes that are extremely problematic and at risk of landslides. Thirty-one percent of the areas have a slope gradient of more than twenty percent (City of Kigali 2013, p. 5). According to the master plan of 2013, it is expected that Kigali will grow to 4.5 million residents in the next two decades. The city is currently moving in an enormous field of tension between high modernization expectations and the immense day-to-day challenges relating to a sufficient supply of living space, food, and infrastructure.

Rwanda has a quite remarkable relief. The watershed between the major Congo and Nile drainage basins runs from north to south through Rwanda. The large Lake Kivu and the Virunga volcano chain, with heights of up to 4,500 meters, are further geographical features. The interior of the country, where Kigali is located, is in turn characterized by a hilly structure, which gave Rwanda the name "land of a thousand hills." Deep valleys were formerly situated between the hills. Over time, they became filled with floating debris, which today gives them flat, swampy ground.

Kigali: inhabited hill
and green wetlands,
2015

Watercourses, related to the surface water—although only in part
on a permanent basis—flow through the wetlands, which possess an
enormous water storage capacity. In Rwanda, their surface amounts
to a total of 77,000 hectares (Kabalisa 2006, p. 15), which corresponds
to nearly three-quarters of the area of Lake Kivu.

Not only the hills, but also the wetlands play
a central role in Rwanda's agricultural supply, since as a result of
their water regime, they allow a third harvest during the longer dry
season from June to September. They are, however, also conducive
to the production of raw materials (clays, sands), and are used as
grassland and for fish farming as well. The wetlands are very diverse
in character. While the German language only has one word for them,
Rwanda's national language, Kinyarwanda, has over twenty (Kersting
2010, p. 80).

▼   The center of Kigali, 2016

▲

The unplanned
settlement of Agatare:
on steep slopes going
down to the Ruenge
wetlands, 2015

Kigali is preparing for its next phase of
growth. The development plans show a clear aim to modernize. Kigali
would like to become a modern metropolis, and sees developing the
financial sector, among other things, as an important future-oriented
field, parallel to strengthening the industry and service sector. As
a result of an administrative reform, the city region was expanded
in 2005 to include an area of 730 square kilometers. Up to now,
only seventeen percent of this is built-up area, while fifty percent is
ranked as unsuitable for construction. Here, the starting situation of
the hills and wetlands once again comes into play: besides the remaining forested areas, a large part of the area not suitable for building comprises hills with very steep slopes (>30%) and wetlands, which
constitute nineteen percent of the total area (City of Kigali 2013).

While earlier planning aimed at partially
draining the wetlands and its urban development, today, their exis-
tential significance for the viability of the city has been recognized.
Adjacent to the central business district, they serve as park and
leisure facilities. The function of the wetlands for the urban metabolism is, at the same time, also becoming increasingly clear. Their ability
to absorb and store water makes them a central co-system to built-
up areas. With their steep slopes and the huge masses of water that
drain off in rainy periods, they are indispensable to the city's water
management. As a result of their storage function and their relatively
fertile soil, they make it possible to harvest several crops each year.
This makes them interesting for agricultural use integrated into the
urban area. For the city, developing agricultural production in parallel
does not fundamentally represent a contradiction to its ambitious
economic goals as East Africa's financial center.

Agricultural use of
wetlands, 2015

Increasing food security is a declared national aim and also includes the city. Today, sixty-three percent of the urban area is still used agriculturally. In addition to increasing production on the areas that remain, integrating small-scale urban agriculture is also an objective. What is shown here is not just a sensitization to urban nutritional issues; this promotion of self-production also corresponds with the great agricultural tradition of the country as well as with acute questions of urban poverty.

What development concepts are appropriate for this starting situation and what kind of infrastructure systems can serve as answers to the specific needs of the location? And furthermore: How can they be implemented successfully? We are currently occupying ourselves with these questions within the framework of a research project addressing the challenges of rapid urbanization from the perspective of infrastructure.

In the Rapid Planning research project, which started in 2014, a broadly interdisciplinary team has been examining how possible synergies between various material flows that are necessary to supply cities can be generated, and which trans-sectoral infrastructure systems are required for this in several cities—along with Kigali. For the first time, the food system here has been included systematically in the canon of urban infrastructures and considered as a central material flow in addition to water, energy, and waste. In contrast to traditional infrastructure systems, food supply is a hybrid, since it is largely organized by the buying behavior of private households, therefore by the market, and thus evades the grasp of urban planning at first glance. There is, however, a range of direct interfaces to urban planning to which attention first has to be given.

For one, in urban growth centers, not only the question of who has access to water is important, but also who has access to food—from a socioeconomic and spatial perspective. How fine is the network of retail outlets and markets, and how does it change along with the urban structure? Second, what food can be produced in the urban region, and can they make a contribution to food security and to the fight against poverty? What spaces are available for this? And third: Can closed-loop economies and links be created, in a different way than today, between material flows, thus facilitating improved resource management?

The project therefore works on parallel levels. On the one hand, existing material flows and infrastructure systems are first comprehended for each sector. In the case of food, in particular, the flows go far beyond the system boundaries of the city. The needs of growing cities influence land use and means of production in rural areas, in the surroundings of the city, in the country, or in other countries. Parallel to this, agricultural manufacturing methods often change in light of goals to increase production as well as a stronger orientation of products for the (world) market. These processes are interdependent. In scholarship, the term "telecoupling" is used for this kind of linkage between social and ecological systems.

The Rapid Planning team has put the focus on cities and is trying to make such linkages visible through describing their resource requirements, differentiated according to socioeconomic units. In a further step, consideration is given to where there are points of linkage between individual flows and whether and/or how they can be organized more effectively within the urban system with respect to resource consumption. This also includes an examination of the interfaces with the agricultural system. The programs and strategies of urban planning and the agricultural sector are still not linked to one another, and each follow a different inherent logic. It is therefore important, with respect to food security, to, on the one hand, take future food requirements into consideration, and, on the other hand, to ask what forms of food production can reasonably be linked with urban development.

In Kigali, in addition to the hilly areas in the north, which are used for traditional agriculture, forms integrated into the city such as agroforestry systems on the steep slopes or modi-

Micro building blocks in the metabolic concept: the farmers' cooperative produces its fertilizer by composting the settlement's organic waste

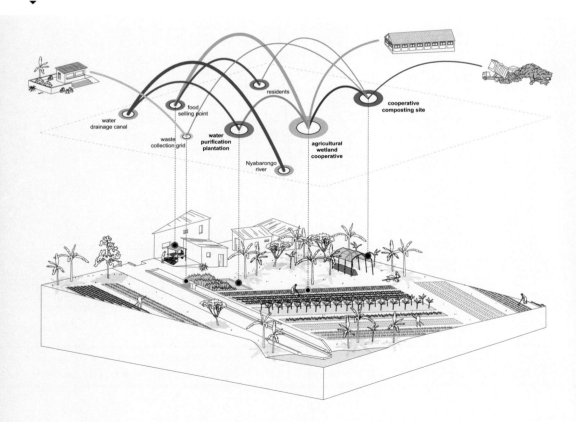

fied vegetable production in the wetlands also play a role. For those it is particularly interesting to consider a link with other material flows, such as water and waste. The premise being that interactive infrastructure systems that activate these interfaces are not purely technical solutions. They are instead links between socioeconomic, natural, and technical systems. In other words: Humans and nature are both likewise actors of the infrastructural system. To examine the extent to which organization can be centralized or decentralized is part of the research project.

It is the middle of November. We are sitting with representatives of the Rwampara Wetland Cooperative in a school in Agatare for a workshop in which we want to address questions regarding the linking of the wetlands with the settlement.

Agatare is located in the Nyarugenge district not far from the center, on the largest hill in the city. It is one of the oldest unplanned settlements of Kigali, and, with eighty-six hectares and 18,914 inhabitants (status 2014), comparatively large. Agatare extends over steep slopes directly down to the wetlands, which is here used primarily for agricultural purposes, among others, by a cooperative of around thirty farmers, who produce vegetables and

Everyday linkage sites: a water kiosk and a collection point for recyclable waste on a small public square
▼

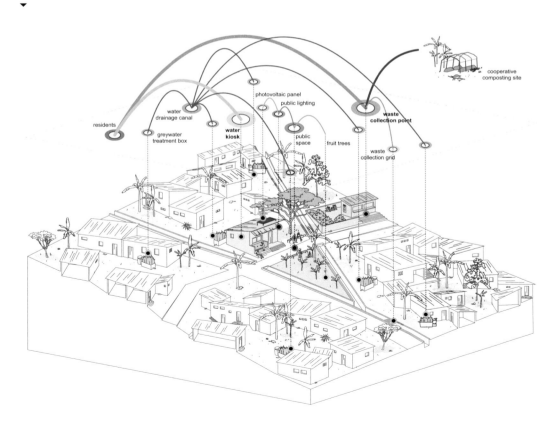

▲ Workshop on a metabolic concept for Agatare, 2016

▲ The water kiosk: overhauled by residents and students during an international summer school, 2015

▲ In the field: problems are discussed with the farmers cooperative, 2015

supply local markets. Except for a few paved streets, Agatare is up to now only accessible via steep footpaths, often parallel to the open drainage system. In line with the urban planning of the City of Kigali in cooperation with the World Bank, the settlement is a first reference project for the preservation and valorization of an informal settlement in Kigali. Since two-thirds of the population of Kigali lives in unplanned settlements, the valorization concept has an exemplary character. In addition to improving supply infrastructure and structural maintenance, it is aimed above all at infrastructural measures, but also includes an expansion of local agricultural activities. Here, the municipal planning can be linked with the action research of the Rapid Planning project and its systemic approach.

It was only a few years ago that the farmers first received the land to be cultivated from the city. They grow vegetables, which they then sell at urban markets. Dairy farming is also practiced to a limited extent. The milk is sold in the neighborhood; the cow manure is used to produce fertilizer. The climate and the steady availability of water make it possible to have three harvests per year. One problem, however, is flooding in the rainy season, which hinders cultivation for several weeks. The work is also severely hampered by the garbage that washes into the wetlands along with the rain via the open water drainage system. Infrastructure planning for Kigali also foresees connecting existing settlements step-by-step with a wastewater system. Such retrofitting is, however, cost-intensive and will take a long time. Another goal is collecting more rainwater and therefore reducing runoff rates.

While we were discussing where possible problem-solving approaches might lie, a heavy rain began. Within a very short period of time, torrential rain was rushing through the erosion channel of the steep school grounds. It was the short rainy season—so we were spared flooding in the classrooms, which is not the case in the long rainy season when the rooms are often submerged in water. We talked with the farmers, but also had workshops with employees of the school and with residents who live along a drainage system. At the end, there was a micro-concept for linking the infrastructure systems. It includes, among other things, the test implementation of cleaning boxes for the gray water of private households, the development of the rainwater storage capacity of the neighboring school, the creation of purchase points for garbage collected separately, the construction of sales points for agricultural products as well as a project to produce more fertilizer for the Wetland Farmer Cooperative by means of compost. The evaluation of activities on the micro-scale flows into the development of further methods for interactive infrastructure.

Kigali faces tremendous challenges. The city shares the immense problems of making affordable living space available and organizing transport with many other urban growth centers. In this brief report, attention focused on the particularity of the unconventional topography. This makes the "groundedness to nature" of the site, in the sense of the Anthropocene, inevitably perceptible. How can linking the city with its hills and wetlands become a generator for a unique city identity and at the same time offer a path-breaking organization of metabolic processes in a rapidly growing urban-natural system? What knowledge is necessary for this, and how can it be generated? What are the drivers and who are the actors in such processes of transformation? Where do blockades lie? With this, we have named only a few of the great challenges, not only for the city, but also for the methods and work practices of landscape architecture.

•

Project data

Project title
Rapid Planning—Sustainable
Infrastructure, Environmental
and Resource Management
for Highly Dynamic Metro-
politan Regions

International research project
supported by the German
Federal Ministry of Education
and Research (BMBF)

Project management
Verband zur Förderung ange-
passter, sozial- und umwelt-
verträglicher Technologien
e. V. (AT-Verband)

Team at TU Berlin
Department of Landscape
Architecture + Open Space
Planning, Prof. Undine
Giseke, Christoph Kasper,
Juliane Brandt, Katharina
Lindschulte, Maria F. Agudelo
Ganem

Other project partners
Brandenburg University of
Technology Cottbus-Senften-
berg (BTU-CS); Frankfurt
University of Applied
Sciences (FRA-UAS); Institut
für Automation und Kommu-
nikation (ifak) Magdeburg;
Institute for Energy and
Environmental Research
(ifeu) Heidelberg; Institute
for Eco-Industrial Analysis
Heidelberg e.V. (IUWA);
Institut für ZukunftsEner-
gieSysteme (IZES) gGmbH,
Saarbrücken; Ostfalia Uni-
versity of Applied Sciences,
Campus Suderburg; Univer-
sity of Stuttgart—Institute
of Energy Economics and
Rational Use of Energy (IER);
Eberhard Karls Universität
Tübingen—Department of
Geosciences; UN-Habitat—
United Nations Human
Settlements Program

Cooperating cities
Da Nang (Vietnam), Kigali
(Rwanda), Asyut (Egypt),
Frankfurt am Main (Germany)

Team Entry Project Kigali
Ifeu Heidelberg, Christin
Zeitz/Bernd Franke; TU
Berlin, Prof. Undine Giseke,
Juliane Brandt; BTU
Cottbus-Senftenberg, Harry
Storch; UN Habitat, Sylvie
Kanimba, Sebastian Lange

Local cooperation partners
Kigali: City of Kigali (CoK),
Abias Mumuhire; District
Nyarugenge, Emanuel
Ingabire; community repre-
sentative, Canisius Gakwaya

Duration
2014–19

Abias Philippe Mumuhire

Kigali is Growing and Challenging

Kigali is one of the fastest growing metropolises in Africa. We expect to have almost around four million inhabitants by 2040. One of the strategies to address the rapid urbanization process was to establish the Kigali City master plan, which drives and helps deal with the future challenges such as an improved transportation system for city dwellers, and notably the shortage of housing for which we have set up a number of programs. Also, as the city grows, we need to secure functioning urban infrastructures such as electricity. Furthermore, we need to provide jobs and food in order to improve living conditions. One of the city goals is to develop Kigali into a hub within Africa. Given the unique characteristics of Kigali, we are on the right track with our policies and project initiatives to pursue the concepts of sustainability and a Green City and make Kigali a livable city.

Rwanda has a unique terrain structure and Kigali in particular has the opportunity to take advantage of these natural conditions. Building on the top of mountains creates views, and we also have the wetlands on the bottom of the hills. This means building capacities for water and drainage systems management. The wetlands have the potential of an ecological neighborhood and we can also create environmentally friendly public parks for recreational use. In addition, most of the agricultural activity takes place in the wetlands, growing food for feeding the people of Kigali.

Preserving the environment has been the key priority of the government. Increasingly, people inhabit the wetlands, which is not a good location because of the threat of flooding; they can get washed away during the rainy season. One the key components of the master plan is to address making the wetlands productive: assigning an area for food production, recreational space, and for water shedding in order to control the water and drainage system, also during the rainy seasons.

Kigali is also characterized by unplanned settlements, Agatare is one of them. The Agatare upgrading programs will have a major impact on the living conditions of the people. The city focuses on safety, accessibility, erosion and flooding reduction by providing intact infrastructures such as an improved drainage systems in order to improve the security of the inhabitants. In terms of accessibility, we will improve street lighting that will make people feel safer and part of the city. What will also help us is retaining the rainwater better, before it runs into the wetlands and causes flooding and damage to the crops there. The goal of the project is to make sure that people live in safe environment at day and night with food security so they can enjoy feeling like part of the community.

The Rapid Planning Project (RP) in partnership with the City of Kigali can be one of the drivers for implementing the visions of the master plan. The RP project links the needs of the people situated on the hills with the needs of the wetlands, which will be key. The Rapid Planning's very good scientific-based research approach is looking at key issues and finds solutions in key areas such as agriculture, waste and water management, and sanitation. Dealing with the Rapid Planning team is very easy and helpful in assisting our community to produce compost and help them use it in their agricultural production. The food produced will also have an economic impact on the City of Kigali, not least in terms of providing jobs in the urban environment, no matter whether they are formal or informal jobs. I think agriculture is a driver in shaping and improving people's lives in the neighborhood. The interaction between the community and the Rapid Planning team is good for building capacity and the know-how transfer in order to help increase productivity in the wetlands.

That is the wish of the Rwandan government: to create a sustainable and dignified environment that reflects the values and the cultural behavior of the Rwandan society.

◆

Regine Keller

Cañada Real Galiana

3   Cañada Real Galiana, Spain
Europe's Biggest Slum

"Nulla si truova insieme nato e perfetto" *
Leon Battista Alberti, 1435

On the Paseo del Prado in Madrid, hundreds of sheep are driven through the city once a year in a great spectacle. This annual event secures the historical right of way of Spanish sheep farmers, since the Paseo is part of a far-reaching network of livestock routes, the so-called Cañadas Reales. Among the general public, however, the name Cañada Real is connected with something quite different than a pastoral landscape route, since it is also the location of the biggest slum in Europe, where 40,000 people live illegally—a conflict that results in major political and urban-planning controversies again and again. The question that arises is whether it might not be possible at this location to unite the historical cultural landscape and the informal growth of the city. Our team of professors has been looking at this question along with students for two years, and is now able to present approaches to solutions by way of master's theses.

◀   The Cañada Real trails through the periphery of Madrid, 2016

*   "Nothing is at the same time both new and perfect."
From: Leon Battista Alberti, *De Pittura*, Libro III, 63

Map of royal livestock
routes in Spain,
ca. 1925

The Cañada Real
Galiana

The renowned merino sheep have been driven
from summer to winter pastures along the picturesque route of the
Cañada Real Galiana since the early Middle Ages. The pastoral landscape routes—resembling an elongated infrastructure network—
span the entire country with a total length of around 125,000 kilometers. A large part of Spain's power was once based on trade with the
valuable wool. From 1273 to 1836, this power was represented by the
Mesta, the association of sheep farmers in Castile. It organized the
so-called *trashumancia,* the migration of sheep—which numbered
some three million around 1500—from Andalusia and Extremadura
to Castile. The Mesta protected its members and was responsible
for maintaining the routes and watering places. In 1273, it was able to
persuade the Spanish King Alfonso X of Castile to guarantee by edict
the existence of the Cañadas Reales in perpetuity—and this edict
is still valid today. The name consists of *cañada* (livestock track) and
real (royal). The individual sections traverse the country in stages of
up to 800 kilometers in length and pass through the most varied rural
and urban regions in Spain along the way. The width of the Cañada
Real was fixed at ninety ells *(varas castellanas),* which equals 72.22
meters. The today mostly still continuous landscape routes are on the
list of prospective UNESCO World Heritage sites. In the meantime,
the distinguishing landscape elements of the Cañada Real such as
resting places *(descansaderos)*, watering places *(abrevaderos)*, stone
shepherds' huts *(chozos),* and buildings for washing the wool *(lava-
deros)* are at risk of being lost due to rapid urbanization.

The Biggest Slum
in Europe

Today, some livestock routes have developed
into recreational routes. However, a much more interesting fact is
that, along the Cañada Real Galiana, the biggest slum in Europe has
developed (Dietz 2014) on a fifteen-kilometer-long section to the
southeast of Madrid. Approximately 30,000 to 40,000 people live
here illegally. Up to now, the region of Madrid has come up with no
clear concept for how to deal with the informal settlement and has
reacted drastically in the past with removing the people living here by
force. Dwellings are simply bulldozed, and the problem is therefore
proverbially pushed further to the outskirts of the city. The case of
the Cañada Real Galiana, with the superimposing of informal urbanization on a historical structure, has been a research subject at the
Chair of Landscape Architecture and Public Space at the Technische
Universität München for more than two years. Based on this example,
we have made it our task to examine the potentials of the landscape
space, the capacity of the historical structure, and the abilities of the

▲ Herd of sheep on the Cañada Real Galiana near Madrid, 2016

residents of the informal settlement in order to elaborate a way for these aspects to coexist by means of a landscape architecture concept. The aim is to illustrate that both—the preservation of the cultural landscape and the unplanned urban growth—need not be mutually exclusive. To do so, we set out on several expeditions to the Cañada Real Galiana, as landscape architects on a search for the livestock route and, in cooperation with ethnographers, in direct contact with the local population.

On the Search for the Royal Sheep

From a distance, the shepherd looks like one expects a herdsman to look: small and somewhat stooped, a man tanned by the weather, leading a mule by the bit. The animal is loaded with the shepherd's belongings. Around the two scurry two herding dogs of different sizes. They obey the call of the shepherd and race down the valley basin lying in front of us to keep the grazing herd of some 400 animals together. So there they are, the sheep we have been looking for over many days and long distances on the

▲ Moroccan garden at the edge of the settlement, 2016

▲ The bosses of the Cañada, 2016

Cañada Real Galiana, one of the many royal livestock routes in Spain. As we approach the herd, I see the shepherd in intensive dialogue with his smartphone. When we reach him, he tells his device that he is no longer alone and snaps it shut. He grins at us, looks curious, asks who we are, and turns out to be very talkative. I had not been expecting that, had actually envisioned a shepherd who was taciturn and introverted. He is pleased by our interest in his work, and we learn various things about his animals, which are kept here as milk stock. The dogs' names are Tania and Miguel, the lady mule answers to the name Maria. When we ask the shepherd more about the transhumance, the seasonal migration, it turns out that he no longer really believes in the existence of the routes: "Those times ended the moment the sheep were transported overland in trains. Today the routes, which are called Via Pecuario here, are enjoyed by leisure cyclists and hikers, and have already no longer been the main place for livestock trails for a long time."

The renowned Paseo del Prado, today the museum promenade in Madrid, is also part of this old network of routes and is celebrated like a public festival each year with the driving of the royal herd of sheep. While we are speaking with the shepherd, a lamb is born, and we become witnesses to how quickly the newborn animal stands on its legs and begins suckling. After fifteen minutes, everything has taken place and the shepherd collects the young animal, to then bring it, piggyback on the mule, along with the herd.

Cañada Informal

Following the traces of these old routes means observing their metamorphosis in unsettled as well as highly urbanized contexts. Many of the livestock routes in rural areas can still be experienced continuously, whereby the old track remains where there is new infrastructure such as airports and highways, with the contemporary road bypassing it. The Cañadas Reales seem the most interesting, however, at the interface to the city, where they, as to the southeast of the Spanish capital, take on unplanned manifestations. On the historical Cañada Real Galiana here, between the municipal areas of Madrid, Rivas, Coslada, and San Fernando, the biggest slum in Europe has come into being. The informal settlement has developed linearly, on a stretch of fifteen kilometers, and not first in the past few years. People have been settling here for over sixty years, either in carefully constructed stone houses or only provisionally carpentered huts. In the north, in the older part of the settlement in San Fernando, the architecture of the buildings in the meantime even displays a more or less regular character. Created at one time from old farm-workers' houses, here, a legalized area, and thus completely connected with the urban infrastructure, has already developed. The houses here already have two to three stories and are surrounded by fences and walls. While the first to settle here were farm-workers from Andalusia and Extremadura, in the phase that followed, there was an influx of Roma from Bulgaria, Romania, Portugal, and Spain. In the most recent phase, the 2000s, during the Spanish building boom, workers from North Africa, above all Moroccans, most of who are of the Muslim faith, came as well. This colorful ethnic mixture constitutes the population of the Cañada Real Galiana today. For the sake of clarity, along the fifteen kilometers, the communities have divided the Cañada into six sectors from the north to the south. In the south, the poorest section, which is located in direct proximity to the city's mountains of garbage, also has the most precarious conditions. Here, people dwell for the most part in huts and shacks and

▼ Lost world in the mountain of rubbish of the Cañada Real Galiana, 2016

search the garbage for recyclable materials. Madrid's hotbed of the drug trade has also developed in this sector. This is also where the city undertakes rigorous demolition measures, thus further exacerbating the situation. The recycling economy in the trash represents an important economic factor for many residents in the south of the Cañada Real Galiana. Since 2015, another ability has become established: Moroccan residents have begun creating gardens to produce their own vegetables on the Cañada.

There has already been a high level of commitment to the residents on the part of NGOs for some years. In the meantime, neighborhood groups that are in the position to provide help in the informal situation—ranging from medical care to Spanish lessons for Moroccan men and women—have formed. Arquitectura Sin Frontera, Todo por la Praxis, and Zuloark are groups of architects that have been involved in the Cañada Real Galiana with individual projects. Starting in 2016, José Antonio Martínez Páramo is the first Comisionado Regional of Madrid, who is supposed to regulate the precarious social and urban planning situation along the Cañada Real Galiana.

On the Search
for People

During multiple stays on the Cañada Real Galiana since 2014, we have been trying, in cooperation with students, to understand and document the situation and the existing potential on site from the perspective of landscape architecture. Extensive analyses of the spatial conditions and numerous conversations with residents have provided multifaceted insights into life on the historical route of the Cañada Real Galiana. The absence of formal planning here has not only set free the residents' talents, thus providing us with information on how people create infrastructures themselves, specifically in places where formal structures break down. What the sociologist AbdouMaliq Simone coined with the phrase "people as infrastructure" (Simone 2004) can also serve in landscape architecture as a key for developing public spaces into informal structures. Thanks to the collaboration with the ethnographers Professor Ignacio Farias and Tomás Criado, we were also able to acquire in-depth insights into the life of people on the Cañada. The sociological survey methods of "photo-elicitation" and "shadowing" also enabled our students to cautiously develop contacts and summarize their experiences in journals, photo documentation, and films, which then formed the basis for designs for the Cañada.

Merced and Miguel

As we were buying a cola from the kiosk that Ibrahim constructed himself, a large transporter came down the bumpy Cañada. The driver stopped directly next to us, rolled down the window, and said unexpectedly: "Hey, if you want, you can visit us at home afterward!" "Us" is him and his wife and two children. "We live in the last house on the trail," he said to us and drove on. When we went looking for the last house on the trail, we found a halfway ruined farm-worker's house, to which a makeshift canopy had been added using wooden posts and planks. We climbed over a mountain of debris that towers in the entrance area, and were warmly greeted by Merced and Miguel. Miguel's face and arms are black, and the rest of the family does not look truly clean either. The young couple lives with its children in and from garbage, and they have been muddling through, for years. The couple's greatest desire: "If we can somehow save the money, we want to build a bathroom out here." "Life is hard here," they say, "but also free." And this unites many residents in the Cañada, just as does the desire to get out of here at some point. And everyone is also united by the constant feeling of not being truly safe here, either from being robbed by others or from having their dwellings demolished by the police.

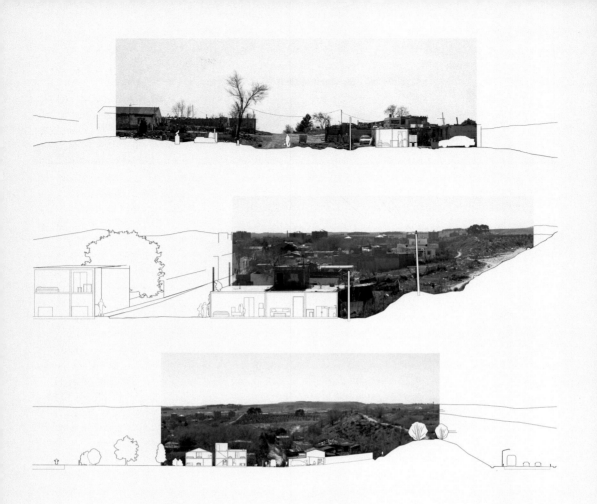

▲
Landscape sections, 2016

Overall plan of the Cañada Real Galiana, Sector 5, 2016
▼

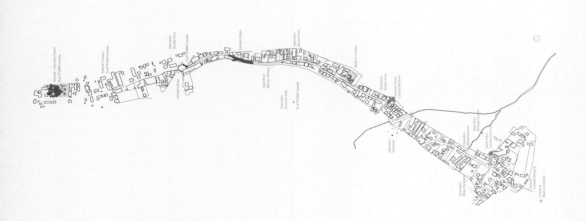

56

Project data

Project title
Cañada Real Galiana, Spain:
Europe's Biggest Slum

Project team
Prof. Dipl.-Ing. Regine Keller,
M. Sc. Johann-Christian
Hannemann, Dipl. -Ing. Felix
Lüdicke (Chair of Landscape
Architecture and Public
Space, TUM); Dr.-Ing. Mark
Kammerbauer

Contracting authority/
Funding body
DAAD-PROMOS, ERASMUS
Program

Cooperation partners
Prof. Dr. phil. Ignacio Farias
Hurtado, Dr. phil. Tomás
Sánchez Criado (Professor-
ship for Participatory Tech-
nology Design, TUM); Prof.
Luis Basabe Montalvo (ETSA
Madrid); Prof. Dr. Daniel
Zarza (Universidad de Alcalá,
Madrid); Fundación Sec-
retariado Gitano; ACCEM;
Families of the Cañada Real;
Goethe Institut Madrid

Students
Susanne Baur, Julian
Birkmaier, Janine van
Bon, Franziska Hepp, Ines
Hoffmann, Yiqun Le, Laura
Loewel, Johanna Rainer

Duration
02/2015—today

Might it be possible to unite the "lives of others" with urban planning ideas so as to create formalized structures here?

Is it conceivable, without a forced resettlement policy, to make the Cañada Real Galiana into a location of reminiscence on its historical origins and a place of further urban development at the same time?

Spatially, the Cañada Real offers an interesting start that could be utilized with respect to urban planning. With its width of 72.22 meters, the historical corridor of the livestock route represents—with the necessary supply infrastructure in the middle—the ideal dimensions for a linear city model. The urbanistic ideas of a "Ciudad Lineal" for Madrid by Arturo Soria y Mata from the year 1882 might resonate here (Fidel 2008).

In it, the structural capacity of the Cañada Real seems to be sketched out almost perfectly. Through taking up this structure, it is conceivable for the livestock route to be protected as a central supply axis, to then legitimize the informal construction situated on the sides of it as a logical addition.

A preliminary proposition that therefore arises is as follows: The valuing of the specific abilities of the residents and the further development of the spatial capacity of the historical structure of the Cañada can result in a viable overall concept in the sense of designing and planning contextually and increase acceptance of the informal settlement. In the best case, the coexistence of the historical livestock route and the settlement lead to an identity-conferring added value rather than an irritation.

Linear City (Ciudad lineal) model of Madrid by Arturo Soria y Mata, 1882

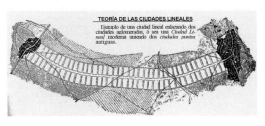

Daniel Zarza

A ▶

10**6**	10**5**	104
1000x1000km	100x100km	10x10kr
10**3**	10**2**	10**1**
1x1km	100x100m	10x10m

"All objects are systems, in the sense that they are formed of many different and interconnected parts, and the fractal dimension describes one aspect of this rule of articulation. But the same definition is just as applicable to artifacts. One difference between natural and artificial systems is that to distinguish the former one must make use of observation or experience, while for the latter one can consult artifice. Doubtless there are very complex artifacts in which so many intentions have come together in so uncontrollable a way that the result ends up as, at least partly, an object of observation."

Benoit Mandelbrot,
The Fractal Geometry of Nature, 1975

Livestock Drove Roads

B ▶

10⁶

The land of the Iberian Peninsula and its rugged central plateau are seamed by nine historic royal drove roads *(cañadas)* seventy-five meters wide and more than 600 kilometers in length.[1] Established by the Mesta (el Honrado Concejo de la Mesta: a sheep ranchers' association)[2] in the Hispanic Middle Ages, they are the physical traces left by Mediterranean transhumance. They are tracks for animals, used for moving livestock between northerly winter pastures and summer grazing in the southern mountains. The drove roads are perhaps one of the oldest elements we know associated with wealth (livestock) and with town and country planning. What was to become a natural landscape was formed by a *network of green ecological corridors* that traversed the arid plateau *(meseta)* with its dryland agriculture, uniting a mosaic of mountain areas of woodland and pasture. The transhumance of livestock having lost its relevance in our country, the drove roads are now protected by the 1995 Livestock Rights of Way Law, and future cultural heritage of UNESCO. Transferring responsibility for them to the Autonomous Communities endows public land with enormous potential in ecological, recreational and social terms.

10⁵

The network of drove roads connects distinct historic regions of the Peninsula. Their very singularity reinforces the distinctiveness of the nation's rich green heritage. Within the two great natural parks of the Guadarrama and Jarama central region two great *drove roads* almost eighty kilometers long resemble *linear green parks or park-like trackways.* Madrid is a distinct central region, the national capital since the time of Philip II, a federal district and metropolitan region. To the north the mountainous areas contribute fundamental water and forestry resources in a wide network of dams and reservoirs in the Tagus basin. To the south the arid chalklands, farmland, and meadows allow natural purification and the transformation of dumps into inselbergs.

10⁴

Metropolitan conurbations are formed through addition to and continuity of pre-existing built spaces, as are city conurbations, urban and suburban peripheries and country towns and villages. So too are empty spaces restructured as complex ones. The former industrial outskirts of Madrid were mostly shaped by informal processes and later incorporated into the city via retrospective legislation and urban transformation. They made it possible for different communities to gain precarious access to housing outside the formal mechanisms (pricing, loans, mortgages, licenses, and permissions, etc.), through self-built housing low in density, site suitability, occupation and building height, the temporary surrender of the use of public land, limited access to services, and a coincidence of rural and urban land use. In today's great metropolis of Madrid, twenty kilometers across and with more than five million inhabitants, the Cañada Galiana is being turned into a green urban landscape adjacent to the southeast metropolitan suburban territory.

A
Scene transitions in leaps in scale of powers of ten

B
Multi-scale view of Iberian livestock routes as human art products between galaxies and atoms as per the powers of ten approach of Morrison, Morrison, Eames and Eames (1982)

1   Cf. http://www.tagesspiegel.de/weltspiegel/gesundheit/ heute-ziehen-wieder-hirten-mit-ihren-schafherden- durch-die-spanischen-canadas/110846.html (accessed November 28, 2016)

2   Cf. "Mesta" in: *The Columbia Electronic Encyclopedia ®;* http://encyclopedia2.thefreedictionary.com/mesta (accessed November 28, 2016)

10^3

The stretch of the Cañada Galiana skirting the southeast region of the metropolis provides forty kilometers of a new *green linear city* with over forty thousand inhabitants. Building morphologically on a former drove road and on an informal basis, with very few rules on the linear structuring of space, makes it possible to create an exceptional district and "rurban" landscape. A landscape that in future will enhance the identity of the capital by recalling traces and memories of a green axis and by regulating urban densities and levels of vegetation. In the process, it includes the solutions to two problems—social informal and ecological—via territorial design appropriate to the richness, diversity, and complexity demanded by metropolitan Madrid as it is today.

10^2

The spatial agglomeration of premises for individual or collective occupation in a mosaic of plots (based on a minimal ranking in economic and accessibility terms) and a network of urbanization (access roads, connection and supply of basic services) are what constitute the essential minima of building a neighborhood, a district, and ultimately a city. The socially diverse Cañada is made up of over a hundred districts or urban blocks a hundred meters square and a hectare in area, each with some thirty plots, maybe fifty family units and about 250 inhabitants. In the urban building morphology of open plots, the public element of the block represents forty and the private element sixty percent (of occupied plots), with a low building density (0.06 ratio of built up space and land area) and environmental values upholding the original green identity of the drove road, organized like a *green boulevard or "rurban" treed avenue* with built areas and landscaped/treed areas in a 36:64% ratio.

10^1

Occupation of the Cañada's seventy-five-meter-wide public strip of the public-heritage land involves occupying and privatizing two strips of verge at the sides, with plots of more or less rigid dimensions, around thirty meters depth and ten of frontage, giving an average surface area of 300 square meters, a width/depth ratio of 1:3, and occupancy levels under thirty percent, leaving *large green gardens and open spaces* and serving to create evolutionary "seeding" housing via an informal initial process that might then be regularized and integrated into the future morphology of the city. This "informal" process is perpetually unfinished, continually in transition right from the first stable entity: the plot. The plot shields itself with a wall for protection and security, and opens itself up to spaces of collective communication by means of intermediate, semi-open spaces linking interior and exterior, like porches and gardens. Increasing flexibility will bring economically productive areas (workshops, shops, kitchen gardens, storage premises, garages, etc.). The self-built cell of "seeding" housing evolves towards more progressive housing, serving as a minimum social and environmental unit and a unit of productivity and exchange.

▲

The Osborne bull by
Manolo Prieto (10^1)
today points the way
on Spanish roads as a
national icon

▲ Trails of plant-eating wandering herds in the Serengeti (10^2)

▼ Real estate development projects lying waste as a result of
the financial crisis juxtaposed with the development of the
Cañada Real Galiana (10^3)

▲

Hippopotamus skin
(10^2) or a bird's-eye
view of the oldest
cultural landscape,
the savanna of
Mesopotamia (10^3)

Johann-Christian Hannemann

Canaan

4   Canaan, Haiti
            New City of Hope
            People, Houses, and the Forces of Nature after
            the Earthquake in 2010

"Goudou Goudou" is what people call the devastating earthquake that killed more than 300,000 people in Haiti in January 2010. Just as many were injured; more than 1.3 million Haitians became homeless from one day to the next. Three years later, the capital of Haiti, Port-au-Prince, still seemed to visitors to be a *bidonville* (shanty town) being engulfed by garbage. This false picture was quickly put into perspective: the city resembled less a destroyed city than one massive construction site. The population was rebuilding its habitat, its city, itself. The state has almost completely withdrawn from people's day-to-day life, and construction of social housing has not been promoted for decades. Three years later, this fact has also changed very little. The building substance has, however, for the most part been reconstructed, and in many places—where the tent camps of the displaced once stood—there are now colorful Creole squares. The growth of unplanned, undersupplied city districts vulnerable to natural hazards, in contrast, has remained unchecked.

Since 2012, students of the Harvard Graduate School of Design, the Leibniz Universität Hannover, and the Technische Universität München (TUM) under the direction of Professor Christian Werthmann and Professor Regine Keller have been addressing the aftereffects of the earthquake on a landscape and urban planning level. From this initiative developed one master's study project in Hannover and the transdisciplinary Urban Strategies for Onaville research group, the focus here, within the context of which the author and TUM students of various chairs have realized their master's theses and done work stays in Haiti since 2013.

◀   Unplanned growth on expropriated territory, 2016

▲

Inaccessible mountain
and marsh landscapes,
ca. 1750

▲

Location of Canaan
in the metropolitan
region of Port-au-
Prince, 2016

Canaan, City of Hope, Built in an Area of Natural Hazards

"Hot, infertile tuff soil. Isolated groups of neem trees and cacti, from which the displaced have wrested squares for their districts. Canaan, a mixture of women, children, and men, of smiles and tears, hunger and thirst. A chaotic collection of blocks of plywood houses and predominantly blue, tarp-covered dwellings stamped with international acronyms, which shot out of the ground like a huge mushroom, climbed quickly from hill to hill, covering them with a network of displaced life.... Here and there were houses created from solid material, which gave the location its topography as an official shantytown of the future. And dust everywhere, in hair, eyes, hands, natal clefts, legs, settled in the most intimate area of life. Canaan, a dry place abandoned by God, that a few hundred disaster victims from the area occupied immediately after the earthquake and proclaimed the Promised Land. One year later, there were, according to a few reliable sources, eighty thousand." *

Destruction in Port-
au-Prince after the
earthquake, 2010
▼

* Kettly Mars, *Vor dem Verdursten*, 2013, pp. 9–10

Aerial view of Canaan, 2016

At the foot of the Mornes du Pensez-y-Bien (also called the Chaîne des Matheux), a barren mountain massif scarred by natural forces and devastation fifteen kilometers north of the capital, a new city is being created. Seven years after the "biggest land seizure in Latin America," more than 200,000 individuals live in Canaan, and more arrive each day. In 2010, a United Nations (UN) refugee camp was set up here on the alluvial cone of the seasonal wild river, Ravine Madaniel. As a result of the expropriation of a territory of around fifty square kilometers, Canaan, which is subject to landslides, floods, storm, and drought, has grown to be the sixth largest city in the country in only six years. While local and national authorities fought against illegal seizure of land and the uncontrolled growth of settlements at the beginning, they were soon tolerated, since neither the state nor the "international community" saw itself in the position to be able to realize formal housing construction at a comparable speed. The lack of regulation manifested in Canaan shows that it is the illegal property market alone that decides how hazard-prone a "new home" is: those who depend on affordable housing live in high-risk areas. But this does not only apply in the case of Canaan and informal settlements. The erection of the UN Corail-Cesseles refugee camp in the area influenced by the Ravine Madaniel as well as new construction projects costing millions on the Zoranje floodplain near the coast show that national and international planning institutions also fall back on constructing housing in at-risk areas—without using construction methods adapted to the circumstances when doing so—due to unclear property ownership structures.

So that undesirable developments like these are not repeated in future, for Onaville—the easternmost neighborhood of Canaan and the one most seriously threatened by possible natural disasters—the transdisciplinary research team set itself the goal of presenting landscape-based alternative planning that takes the altered social circumstances into consideration.

Unplanned settlements in natural hazard zones in Port-au-Prince, 2013
▼

Onaville-en-Haut, 2013
▼

Corrugated metal huts and drainage ditches in deeper-lying areas of Onaville, 2016

River bank of Ravine Madaniel and stone masonry work, 2014

Terraced steep slope and obstructed drainage channels, 2016

The Context Makes the Difference: The Alluvial Cone, People, and Their Everyday Practices

The questions that arise from the objective named relate primarily to how landscape- and neighborhood-based planning strategies might look in the first place: Is it possible in Onaville, and Canaan, to arrive at urban planning that is adapted to the context, and in which the respective cultural landscape, natural processes, and "people who build themselves" are no longer ignored? Would it instead be possible to begin on the basis of intensive basic research and sensitively coordinated planning interventions as well as with imparting hazards and potentials? Might uncontrollable urbanization tendencies in Canaan thus be steered to a certain extent and the vulnerability of people and their city to natural catastrophes be reduced?

The site of contemporary Canaan, except for a few favorable locations where sugarcane, indigo, and sisal were grown, was already in the mid-eighteenth century regarded as wild, inaccessible terrain *(pays inabordable)*—characterized by the stony, infertile steep slopes of the Montagne du Pensez-y-Bien, which were used for animal breeding and charcoal burning, and the floodplain of the Rivière Boucan Brouc. Today, more than 10,000 people live in Onaville on the approximately nine-square-kilometer-large alluvial cone of the Ravine Madaniel and adjacent steep slopes.

Until today, the mostly dry riverbed of the Madaniel is used as infrastructure. TapTaps—pick-up trucks converted into small buses—drive on it to transport people and their belongings to higher-lying neighborhoods; trucks bring building materials from illegal quarries down to Canaan, while residents answer the call of nature in the seasonal wild streams, using them as "self-cleaning" rubbish dumps. The rocks of the ravine serve stonemasons as a resource: In short, powerful blows of the hammer, they process them into building materials of different granulations, which they then sell. Steep slopes are terraced with a hoe by hand for homes; but the risk of landslides and erosion then rises as a result of the damage to the grass cover. Others build directly in drainage channels.

The vulnerability of the people is increasing with the growing number of new arrivals: most new settlers lack knowledge of the territory and its hazards; others accept the natural perils as a rare evil determined by chance, since they simply cannot afford more favorable locations.

As the stories of Edali, Pierre, and Alexis show, the day-to-day struggle for a sufficient supply of water, food, work, and education leaves little room for precautionary measures. Edali and Pierre were part of the first wave of settlers. Pierre (a seventy-four-year-old unemployed truck driver) and his wife, Edali (a sixty-four-year-old housewife) live with their twenty-two-year-old son, who studies in Port-au-Prince, on seventeen square meters of a temporary shelter provided by the aid organization TECHO. When the earthquake destroyed their rental apartment in Pétionville in 2010, the family fled to Onaville and purchased a small plot of land "for little money" from one of the committees that sells land illegally. They sealed their hut against the wind using tarpaulins that had served them as a dwelling after the earthquake, while other tarpaulins were recycled to make a fence and a cooking hut; they have also laid out a kitchen garden. Drinking water and water for other uses—as is true for all the residents of Onaville—has to be purchased expensively in buckets *(bokits)* from privately run water kiosks supplied by tank trucks. A latrine in the nearby surroundings is shared with three other families.

Unlike Edali and Pierre, Alexis was not able to afford a plot of land on safe terrain. When Alexis moved to Onaville after his house in Delmas was destroyed, due to rising property pric-es and a lack of financing options, he bought a tiny plot on the eastern slope with its risks of landslides and hurricanes. He terraced his plot and built his shanty of wood and tarpaulins on it. Seven years after the earthquake, Alexis has still not received any help.

Both fates show how severe unemployment, scarcity of financing, and insecurity dominate the reality of the res-idents' lives—a TECHO survey of 2012 revealed an adult unemploy-ment level of nearly ninety percent in Onaville. This and precarious employment relationships result in families generally having to keep house with 1.50 to 3.00 euros per day. A large percentage of this is used for water, food, and transportation.

Students as Assisting Planners of Development from Below

In the past five years, the site analyses of the Urban Strategies for Onaville research group elaborated hydro-geographical and socio-spatial contexts for this neighborhood. To do so, the students cooperated with volunteers from the nonprofit youth organization TECHO Haiti and with residents in Onaville. What stood in the foreground in the process was finding out how communicable descriptions of the natural hazards might flow into simple concepts and improvement strategies for the new city and its environment by means of an iterative process of thinking, acting, and reflecting. Unlike in the case of "helicopter planning" by government and international organizations, the focus was on supporting "development from below." This also meant jettisoning customary research methods.

In the presentation of a modeling of flood risk that was generated by environmental engineering students, it became clear that, to sensitize people, various forms of communication and measures would have to be utilized. In the case of experts, being confronted with the modeling method and the most important facts and flood risk maps suffices. However, to make the same contents accessible to a group of leaders, interested residents, and TECHO volunteers in Onaville, in contrast, means of communication such as plans, maps, and diagrams had to be translated into a form of representation and workshops that could be understood by laypersons and illiterate individuals.

Afterward, the students' fieldwork was oriented in such a way that it was possible, through inspections of locations and neighborhood meetings, to elaborate applied knowledge on natural hazards and mitigation strategies in cooperation with residents.

◀

Alexis's hut, 2016

Alexis with his radio
as his most important
source of information,
2016

What thus became clear is the need for
a local awareness-raising campaign and an early warning network
in the case of catastrophes. The students were able to initiate
both activities in 2014, which were then continued by a local focus
group in the form of providing information to two hundred households threatened by natural hazards. To counter the loss of contextual knowledge and promote self-help, the local actors were also
networked with actors on a national level. Back in Germany, it was
possible to revise the flooding study based on more precise digital
terrain data and to supplement it with components of engineer-
ing-, agroforestry-, and landscape-architecture-related prevention
strategies. Since then, the early warning network organized by the
neighborhood was twice able to prove its importance: Volunteers
activated the inhabitants of Onaville and Canaan in October 2016 in
order to make early emergency provision for the arrival of Hurricane
Matthew. Matthew turned out to be the strongest tropical cyclone

Students cooperate with residents and TECHO volunteers, 2014

Discussion of natural hazards on site, 2014

Awareness-raising campaign for the focus group, 2014

Elaboration of an emergency plan, 2014
▼

to hit Haiti in fifty years, devastating large swaths of land in the southwest and northwest.

Landscape-Based Planning Knowledge for More Sustainable Development

The fact that this kind of fundamental research and strategy development is necessary and in demand in transdisciplinary field and lab work also becomes clear elsewhere: surveys conducted by the master's students were used in 2016 as a basis for planning the fourteen-million-dollar Canaan Upgrading and Community Development program. To what extent the pilot project, whose focus area is outside of Onaville, will be capable of realizing an integrated management of natural hazards as well as preventive protection and development strategies seems questionable in light of the settlement size of Canaan and the duration of only two years.

Canaan has the potential to relieve the capital, which is faced with gridlocks in supply and traffic. When considered as a whole, vast areas of the landscape space offer good prerequisites for future-oriented urban development: exposure to natural hazards is lower in moderate hillside locations and in large areas of the alluvial cone of Onaville than on the steep slopes of Port-au-Prince or the lowlands of the Plaine du Cul-de-Sac, which is confronted with the risk of tsunamis and floods. To react to people's most urgent needs, it is therefore necessary near-term to promote more stable employment opportunities through concentrated action and to further develop public supply facilities. To make Canaan more livable and more resistant to natural disasters, it is nonetheless also necessary to develop land-use concepts and anticipatory strategies that are adapted on the basis of the abilities of residents and their local practices.

▶

A public square
designed by local
initiative, 2013

The residents of Onaville are already providing examples of how this new urban landscape might look: in the last few years, they have planted thousands of trees on new, public squares and in private gardens. The question of whether communal replanting, also beyond strict neighborhood monitoring, can be a successful strategy for repairing degraded slopes and catchment areas and making them usable naturally has to remain open. Nevertheless, communal protection of areas exposed to natural hazards through valorizing them supported by public funds and private actors does appear to be the only promising strategy, when residents of the new city and their individual and collective interests are intensively integrated.

In the view of the research group, it is precisely here that academic work can and must begin because of its relative freedom from financial and political opportunism: complex relationships have to be decoded and new tools, methods, and strategies must be developed. Protection concepts and densification and consolidation strategies have to be designed and negotiated so that house gardens and communally used open spaces can also have a perspective in a consolidated city, without immediately being sacrificed to the property market. These urbanization tendencies and their effects on people and the environment have to be countered with possible alternatives for contextually adapted, livable urban landscape development in Canaan. The positive plans and visions for the future that arise can, in turn, be discussed again with residents and local and national actors. The next generation of students is therefore already working on this future. Since many residents in Onaville share one desire: they are looking for a better life in the city—with their own home and garden.

Since all of this requires a lot of time, continuity, and long-term cooperation with local actors—in our case with grassroots organizations such as TECHO Haiti—it is perhaps only universities that are in the position to tackle tasks of this scale.

In light of increasing local and global migration movements, caused by climate change, war, catastrophes, structural poverty, constructive and site-specific handling of the complex phenomena of planned and unplanned cities will also become a topic of growing importance in Europe and Germany. The example of the informally organized Urban Strategies for Onaville research group shows that students are able to make very important and necessary contributions to real projects and social discussions by means of inter- and transdisciplinary collaboration and great personal commitment, also without financial support.

Project data

Project title
Canaan, Haiti: New City of Hope

Project team
Prof. Dipl.-Ing. Regine Keller, M. Sc. Johann-Christian Hannemann (Chair of Landscape Architecture and Public Space, TUM); Prof. Dipl.-Ing. Christian Werthmann (TUM-IAS Hans Fischer Senior Fellow/Leibniz Universität Hannover); Dr.-Ing. Wolfgang Rieger (Chair of Hydrology and River Basin Management, TUM); Prof. Dr. rer. nat. habil. Brigitte Helmreich (Chair of Urban Water Systems Engineering, TUM); Dr.-Ing. Franz Zunic (Chair of Hydraulic and Water Resources Engineering, TUM); Prof. Dr. Dr. Michael Weber (Chair of Silviculture and Forest Planning, TUM); Prof. Dipl. arch. ETH Mark Michaeli (Chair of Sustainable Urbanism, TUM)

Contracting authority/ Funding body
DAAD-PROMOS, TU München Development Cooperation

Cooperation partners
Prof. Dipl.-Ing. Christian Werthmann (TUM-IAS Hans Fischer Senior Fellow/Leibniz Universität Hannover); TECHO Haïti; Haut-Onaville & Bas-Onaville work group; Viva Rio Haiti; ONU Habitat Haiti; Potentiel3.0 & Communauté OpenStreetMap Haiti; IOM; DroneAdventures; DLR
Students
Bjarne Bächle, María Alejandra Casanova, Raphaela Guin, Johann-Christian Hannemann, Valentin Heimhuber, Ines Hoffmann, Göcke Iyicil, Sean Kerwin, Wolfgang Krötzinger, Nelly Puren

Duration
10/2012—today

Gerardo Gazmuri

Experiences of Participation in Haiti

In 2012, with some experience of social projects within Chile, I applied for a post as volunteer architect with América Solidaria, an organization that works to overcome poverty in various countries of Latin America and the Caribbean. The project, in conjunction with CARE International in Haiti involved leading the processes of work supervision and worker training for housing reconstruction in Carrefour, a commune close to Port-au-Prince that had been severely affected by the earthquake of January 2010.

Consequently, I found myself in a country totally other than my own, with a different culture, a different language, and different rhythms of life. One needed a certain sensitivity to face that reality.

For instance, we, as architects can define how a project for housing reconstruction after an earthquake should proceed. And for me, a Chilean, it is normal to talk of earthquakes and reconstructions, because I come from a country where all sorts of natural catastrophes constantly occur. But in situations where it is particularly important to come up with solutions quickly, then many aspects of the problem can fall outside the ambit of the analysis, and the risk arises of the initiative coming unstuck or of making the situation much worse. Very often outside volunteers do not know how the people live and how they occupy their land: and these are factors that will determine a project's success or failure.

After a year of learning Haitian Creole, talking daily to affected families, hearing their stories and carrying out reconstruction projects, I had managed to gain a clearer view of the situation, and hence to understand what my role in Haiti was.

Already four years had passed since the earthquake, and many international cooperation organizations, including our own, were still seeing Haiti as

Construction training 2013. The program focused on training 250 women from the Carrefour area in building and installation

Handing over emergency housing, Cabaret, 2014. Buildings of eighteen square meters quickly built from lightweight material, 2014

Participatory Rural Appraisal in La Digue, 2014. A process of consultation and interaction with the community carried out via focus groups

Building the Library in Royal, 2014. A "Konbit" is a communal process that aims to achieve a common goal with the aid of all the members of the community

Inauguration of the Library in Royal, 2014

a country in a state of catastrophe. However, the government requested the organizations to move on from an emergency to a development footing, so promoting medium- and long-term initiatives and investments and sustainable solutions.

At this juncture (2014) I had finished my year of professional volunteering with América Solidaria and CARE-Haiti and began work as Director of the Construction Department at TECHO, an organization working in nineteen countries in Latin America and the Caribbean that was also seeking to overcome poverty through joint action with a country's inhabitants, young volunteers (mostly from the country involved), and professionals wanting to work for a more just society.

In its first phase of work TECHO-Haiti had delivered over 2,500 emergency dwellings as an immediate solution to the precarious living conditions; following the guidelines proposed by the government, it now began the second phase of its work, implementing a model of intervention focused on community development, thus assuring the sustainability of its projects.

In this phase TECHO set up a Work Committee in each of the six communities where it operated (La Digue, La Hatt, Royal, Gariche Prince, Onaville-en-Haut, and Onaville-en-Bas) where volunteers and local leaders held periodic organization and participation sessions, understanding each other's roles and abilities, widening their support networks, and building up social capital, joining with neighbors to foster sustainable schemes of individual and collective interest.

This vision of TECHO's, along with my own previous experience, brought me to understand the importance of "participation" in the architectural sphere as a tool for beating poverty and a driver of social change.

At TECHO Haiti, implementing a Participatory Rural Appraisal (PRA) was indispensable; its main purpose was to bolster the community's own resolve by means of "interactive participation" in every phase of a project. Reaching this level of participation meant involving everyone connected with the project—men, women, and children all included—and focusing on shortcomings in the community infrastructure so that, with the help of a set of tools and techniques, the community could make its own analysis and then start to manage the project's planning and implementation, thereby encouraging a sustainable development.

By the use of PRAs, TECHO uncovered significant public infrastructure gaps in the communities where it had been working that affected communal life, limited interaction, and hindered the consolidation of a communal identity, all of which could be developed through adequate infrastructure.

So, it was in response to these shortcomings that TECHO-Haiti's Community Infrastructure Program emerged, offering communities the chance to develop, with expert help, schemes not only for solving one or more problems identified within the community but also boosting local solidarity, social cohesion, and community ownership.

An example of this was a small library in Royal, a rural community of some 300 people about twenty-five kilometers from Port-au-Prince. This was built in 2014 to a participatory design, and one saw the whole community working in unison to achieve the goals they themselves had set. Everyone carried out their role in the project—some performing construction tasks; others preparing food; children and young people ferrying materials or carrying out educational activities—in a common enterprise traditionally known as "Konbit."

In this fashion, we successfully carried out a number of different projects like the Library in Royal: building community plazas in Gariche Prince and La Hatt; installing street lighting and signage in Onaville; elementary schools in La Digue and Gariche Prince, water and sanitation systems in La Hatt and Royal, a multipurpose games court in Gariche Prince, and various social and educational programs that give each of these projects sustainability.

Today I view with pride the achievement of the projects that resulted from this methodology for diagnosing and empowering communities, along with the TECHO team, to build their own dreams.

▸ Inauguration of the Primary School in La Digue, 2014

▸ Volunteers on an emergency housing building day, Cabaret, 2014

Jörg Rekittke

Bali

5

Bali, Indonesia
**Where Twelve Million People Are Transforming
Irrigation into Wastewater**

Bali, Indonesia, is regarded as the "Hawaii of the Indian Ocean" and marketed with pleasure as a premium destination for freshly married couples on their honeymoon. From the perspective of environmental protection, urban planning, and landscape architecture, however, the supposed dream island—without giving too much away—is an ecological nightmare. To be able to show this in a professionally substantiated way and make it visible by means of a sober external point of view, without moralistic finger pointing, as well as indicate possible consequences, we, teachers and students in the Master of Landscape Architecture Program of the National University of Singapore, dedicated an academic studio, an expedition—and now part of our contribution to the exhibition in Munich—to Bali. As the title of our studio, we selected "Bottomless Bali," and as the subtitle added: "A research expedition to an endless city without infrastructure." We were already familiar with the extreme environmental challenges of booming Southeast Asia from numerous projects and fieldwork operations, having dedicated our-selves to the megacity Jakarta for many years in a row, and now wanted to see whether the rapidly urbanizing, exemplary island of Bali—visually the complete opposite of Jakarta—might also be counted among those examples that are characterized by a nearly total lack of wastewater and other environmentally relevant urban infrastructure.

◀   From the mountains to the coastal plains: Bali's rice
terraces—here in Canggu—with their elaborate irrigation
system. The tourist idyll deceives, since the beautiful
landscape has been created as a result of the arduous work
of farmers, 2015

Location of the Island of Bali in the Bali Sea, Indonesia. On the left of the graphic, the eastern edge of Java; on the right edge, the westernmost point of the Island of Lombok. Marked in red is Canggu, our specific area of study, 2015

Pushing your own gas grill through the landscape is indispensable when the imported steak for the barbecue with imported friends is supposed to taste just as good as in Singapore, Sydney, or Stuttgart, 2015

We come uninvited and are not necessarily welcome. From left to right: Philip Paar and Jörg Rekittke with camera drones, on the way back from Ecco Beach. The athletic "surfer dude's" look requires no comment, 2015

The population of Bali currently consists of 4.3 million people. Every year an estimated three million Indonesians and some five million foreign tourists visit the island, with an upward tendency. Bali is located in the Malay Archipelago— a good reason for us to begin our work by reading the book *The Malay Archipelago: The Land of the Orang-Utan and the Bird of Paradise* by Alfred Russel Wallace (1823–1913), a British naturalist, explorer, geographer, anthropologist, and biologist. His name is still known today, since he developed his own theory of evolution based on natural selection. His scientific approach to this topic was published in 1858 along with various texts by Charles Darwin, which, in turn, spurred Darwin to publish his own thoughts as a book—*On the Origin of Species* (1859). Wallace went on extensive voyages in the Malay Archipelago, where he, among other things, identified the eponymous Wallace Line, which designates the biogeographic border that marks the furthermost distribution of Australian fauna in the Malay Archipelago. The area located to the west of the line is characterized by the animal world of Asian origin. Wallace was undoubtedly a great explorer, but his private trade in preserved animals or taxidermy—which manifested itself in the shooting of excessive numbers of birds, orangutans, and other species as well as in the collecting and preserving of insects on a mass scale—contributed to financing his travels. He occasionally did so much shooting in his surroundings that he later reported a total lack of individual species within his field of action.

Unlike the otherwise Muslim-majority Indonesia, the majority of Bali's population adheres to the Hindu-Dharma religion, the Balinese form of Hinduism, which found its way to the island in the 8th and 9th century. The Balinese comprehend the island as a tripartite macrocosm consisting of overlapping spheres. The peaks of the mountains and everything

above them form the realm of the gods.
Under the ground is the realm of dark powers
and demons. In between lies the sphere of
humans. This religious-cultural systematic is
also reflected in the agricultural organization
of Bali. Wallace was already overwhelmed
by the beauty and sophistication of the island
and in his book went so far as to compare
Bali's extensive and lush rice fields with their
elaborate irrigation system to the "best
cultivated" regions of Europe, of which Euro-
peans were quite proud at the time. In Bali,
temples accompany and mark various hierarchy levels—the spatial proximity to the
realm of the gods defines the size and importance of the temple—in the cooperative
irrigation system. This is traditionally organized in the form of *subak,* collectives for
maintaining the irrigation system. Within
a *subak,* farmers meet at regular intervals at
the most important point in their irrigation
section and discuss plans and problems.
A temple is also located there. Where modern times have not already created gaps in
the system, priests and farmers also continue
to jointly monitor the flow of water and the
amounts of water in the rice fields of the
island-wide *subak* system. The logic of such
a highly complex water and/or rice culture
is fascinating—water knows only one natural
direction of flow. It is, however, quite difficult for the fascinated observer to imagine
the elaborate creation of hydrological infrastructure required and the total transformation of the natural landscape by human
hands. Bali's rivers spring forth in the mountains, the realm of the gods, and are channeled into the sophisticated irrigation system
that extends through the realm of human
beings by means of weirs. The main irrigation
canals are laid out along the crest of the
respective section of terrain, generally
corresponding to the position of the roads
on whose left and right sides they are situated. This typology leads to a common
misconception among all non-farmers. They
believe that they have trenches of dirty

▲

The aerial photos taken with a camera drone
clearly show how villas, apartments, and
chlorinated pools are eliminating the traditional
cultivated landscape of Canggu, 2015

▲

House after house is swiftly punched into the
mud of the rice terraces. Directly into the mud,
without creating any form of urban infrastructure
that might serve the purpose of regulated wastewater disposal or contemporary environmental
protection.

▼

The new Bali: Western, sporty, solvent, 2015

water in front of them rather than clean irrigation canals. In the next level of hierarchy, the water is routed to the rice terraces, where it slowly flows downhill and is absorbed by the rivers again at the lowest point. The rivers flow into the ocean, where dark powers and demons frolic. Village inhabitants, traditional rice farmers, mostly keep their distance from the sea. Hindu rituals occasionally take place on the beach, and old cemeteries are also found there. The dead are on a journey into the depths. Influenced by culture, what comes into being along the coast is an area that—from a non-Hindu perspective—represents a kind of use vacuum, which the tourism industry was therefore able to take by storm—without appreciable resistance.

Tourists do not believe in demons; they surf the waves of the warm ocean. They also hardly notice the rice farmers, who continue working as hard as in ages past. What are of interest are the visually incredibly beautiful rice terraces that the farmers cultivate. The intact, agricultural landscape is currently experiencing a veritable invasion of visitors and settlers. Bali was already touted as an exotic paradise in colonial times. However, the most cataclysmic thing that ever befell the island was the cinema release of the embarrassing film *Eat, Pray, Love* (2010), with Julia Roberts in the starring role. Since then, Bali has been overrun by masses of people of international provenance, trying to stabilize their educated, middle-class midlife crisis largely by means of surfing, drinking, motorcycle riding, and yoga. None of them intends to do harm. People show an interest in culture—although not a few live with the assumption that Bali is a Buddhist (rather than a Hindu) culture, which somehow also fits better within the global yin and yang cliché. A healthy lifestyle is called for, and someone does ultimately have to save the world with his money. Money is invested in the construction of real estate; both local and international investors want to own and build a piece of the alleged paradise. So-called villas, apartments, hotels, surf shops, and yoga centers, plus an endless number of swimming pools dominate the building boom. To be able to study this unbridled urbanization dynamic, as the destination for our expedition, we selected Canggu, a village near the coast that is north of urban Seminyak, which has been completely overrun by tourism, and south of well-known Tanah Lot. Canggu also represents an around eight-kilometer-long stretch of coast that is bordered in the south by the village of Berawa, and in the north by the village of Cemagi, and within which prominent surfing spots such as Ecco Beach are located. Canggu is booming and can currently be read like an open book of unrestrained, superfast urbanization. We did so, according to our academic credo of conducting research work without necessarily having been requested, commissioned, or invited to do so. A look at more recent housing development in Canggu shows that it was still a nearly pure farming village until the mid-1990s. The first villas and other forms of tourist accommodations first arrived in 2002—the year when the fatal "Bali bombings," a terrorist bomb attack, resulted in a temporary slowdown in the tourism boom.

In 2009, it was possible to identify a nearly 50:50 ratio between locals and outsiders; in 2015, the year of our expedition, global migrants had long since taken over. There is hardly a single rice field that does not boast a "for sale" sign; real estate agents are celebrating with a huge party, and, ultimately, the whole landscape is up for sale. Every new building is positioned in such a way that it frames the living-room and/or terrace view perfectly on the rice terraces that remain, also when this can often only be achieved by turning the entire building. Soon, the last rice field in Canggu will also have disappeared, making it impossible to produce the individual optical illusion anymore.

We will let others complain about this luxury problem. What interests us are the technique and the consequences of the current transformation of the land. This begins with the sale and then letting the section of the rice terrace fall into disuse. If for-eigners buy they are able to build on the land, but do not truly own it. For that, foreigners need a local straw man. No problem in a nation such as Indonesia, where nobody would dare deny the deeply rooted corruption. The next step is the drawing of a very simple building

The graphic is supposed to show that the new urban develop-ment (New Bali) calls for an independent wastewater system (New Subak), which would need to be constructed from scratch and cannot be allowed to have an impact on the existing, tradi-tional irrigation system, 2015
▼

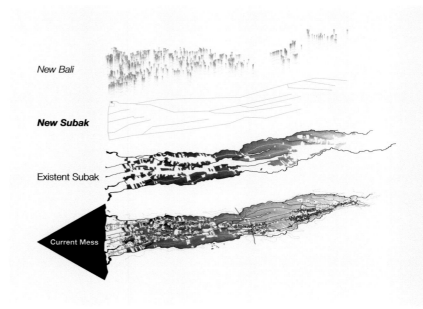

New Bali

New Subak

Existent Subak

Current Mess

The drawing documents a yoga center in Canggu, all of whose wastewater is discharged untreated into an irrigation channel (right). From the irrigation channel, the water that has been discharged is distributed in the surrounding rice fields, 2015

Canggu's settlement boom. Satellite image mapping (based on a Google timeline) of the development of the settlement, divided up according to traditional village structures (black) and newly constructed villas, hotels, and other structures for tourists and new settlers (red), 2015
▼

plan, which the penniless migrant laborers who build the houses of affluent clients also have to be able to read. House after house is then swiftly punched into the mud of the rice terraces. Directly into the mud, without creating any form of urban infrastructure that might serve the purpose of regulated wastewater disposal or contemporary environmental protection. This standardized insanity is shown based on three examples from the results of our expedition.

On his travels, Wallace always began his search for items to study and collect in the direct surroundings of his current accommodations. We followed in his footsteps and first considered our own situation. On the pool terrace of our four-star apartments built by Spanish owners, we enjoyed an idyllic view of green rice fields. At the foot of these rice terraces, we had the chance to precisely study the typical building process on the next site on which

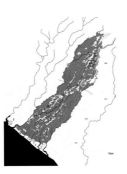

1992   2002   2009   2015

83

one of the innumerable apartment complexes was being built—
in this case by an Australian owner. We got our hands on a copy of
the plan for executing the project. This plan includes absolutely no
wastewater facilities, and they were, according to the foreman of the
constructions site, also not built. On the terrace side of these apartments is a river, into which both toilet wastewater and all bathing
and kitchen wastewater is discharged untreated. Back at our pool,
we followed the wastewater flows in our "luxury accommodation."
All our wastewater—fecal matter, cleaning chemicals, et cetera—is
discharged directly into the rice terraces situated before us by means
of visible plastic pipes. There, it follows the slope until it is washed
into the sea by one of the rivers, insofar as it does not seep into the
soil and the groundwater. What we found most striking is that the
highly chlorinated wastewater from all the pools we saw is also discharged directly into the rice cultivation and the nearest rivers. After
these first random samples, we knew what we had to look for. All
the other construction sites and dwellings—we divided up to cover
the entire area of Canggu—confirmed our worst fears. There are a
couple of septic tanks as well as a well-intentioned attempt to remove
a bit of garbage, but otherwise everything that would actually have
to be absorbed by a municipal network of infrastructure and disposed
of in an environmentally friendly way finds its way into the landscape,
the soil, the groundwater, the rivers, and the sea. We once again took
a closer look at a popular yoga center in Canggu's village area. In
the entrance area of the facility, which is primarily frequented by a
Western clientele, is a shop that sells ecologically correctly produced
food and politically correct local coffee. All the yoga community's
wastewater—fecal matter, cleaning chemicals, simply everything—
is, however, discharged untreated into an irrigation canal from which
the rice that the yoginis and yogis eat receives water.

       If one bears in mind that Bali has to cope
with the wastewater of a total of more than twelve million people
per year, it becomes clear that the splendid irrigation system is being
collectively raped and abused as a wastewater system. We have
stepped up to point out this sacrilege—but we cannot end it. Our
studio also provided no short-term design solution—how could it—
but we believe we are in the position to show that any necessary
change cannot be expected on the part of an ignorant and corrupt
administrative caste, but can instead only be effected by those who
cause the problem themselves. We are moreover sure that our forensic research work shows that further abuse of the irrigation system
can only be prevented if a still-to-be-developed, new, and completely
autonomous wastewater network is built, decoupled from the existing agricultural irrigation network. It might sound obvious and very
trivial, but it means gigantic design tasks in the future. We propose
the creation of a kind of "new subak"—*subak baru*—which does not
irrigate the landscape, but instead relieves the growing urban land-

scape of the masses of wastewater. At the deepest points of the respective new *subak* section, near the coast, where the wastewater from the corresponding areas flows together, wastewater treatment plants have to be constructed, in this case, hopefully, of a Western ecological and technical standard. This is the only way that it is possible to feed treated, non-pathogenic water back into the sea. We will continue working on the topic, but first—and presumably still for a very long time—what applies without restrictions: Come to Bali and swim in your own excrement.

●

Project data

Project title
Bottomless Bali (Bali Studio 2015, head: Jörg Rekittke)

Project team
Prof. Dr. Jörg Rekittke, Philip Paar, Yazid Ninsalam

Contracting authority/ Funding body
the Studio was embedded in the Under-the-Urban-Canopy 3-D research project led by Jörg Rekittke. Financed with funding from the National University of Singapore

Cooperation partners
Sarah Westropp, Bobocha, Siladen Island, Indonesia; Master of Landscape Architecture Program, Department of Architecture, School of Design and Environment, National University of Singapore

Students
Goh Weixiang, Feng Yuanqiu, Xu Haohui, Hu Zhijie, Kow Xiao Jun, Loh Peiqi, Xu Lanjun, Wan Jing, Chow Zhaoyu Jaden, Uraiwan Songmunstaporn, Zhang Shangyu, Xu Yan

Duration
08/2015–12/2015

Jörg Rekittke

Jakarta

6

Jakarta, Indonesia
Where Twenty-Eight Million People Sleep in
Thirteen Riverbeds

Only few cities in the world can hold a candle to Jakarta with respect to the sheer size, the urban challenges to be overcome, and the environmental conditions, which can only be described with difficulty. Approximately ten million people live within the actual city limits, but it is a total of twenty-eight million that make up the megacity Jakarta—with a sharply rising tendency. For 2020, around thirty-five million people are forecasted for the urban territory of the Southeast Asian giant—figures whose exact details are largely irrelevant, since precise censuses have long since become impossible. What is concerned is a truly huge and extreme city—that much is sure. The main part of Jakarta is located in a delta formed by the estuary area of thirteen tropical rivers that flow into the Java Sea. Jakarta can be compared with a slowly, but steadily sinking ship in a permanent storm. The sea level is rising implacably, the ground on which the city is built is sinking with dramatic speed, and heavy rain events, which result in unprecedented flood peaks for the thirteen rivers that run through the city, are becoming more intensive on a measurable scale in the course of changes in the climate. At some places in the urban area, the ground is subsiding up to twenty-five centimeters per year, therefore, one whole meter in only four years. The rate of the land subsidence is scarcely graspable, but this should come as no surprise in light of the millionfold uncontrolled and abusive extraction of groundwater by means of self-drilled well holes with plastic piping and the unstable, soft earth of the delta, which has no means of countering the quickly growing weight of the city. The consequences of the fatal combination of the problematic factors described are revealed to the residents of the city in the form of regular flood events of catastrophic proportions, which—in light of the rapidly increasing settlement and densification—is absolutely impossible to arrest in its tracks.

◀   The Ciliwung River in the area of the district of Kampung
Bukit Duri, Jakarta, Indonesia, 2011

The biggest flood measured in the history of Jakarta took place in February 2007. Around sixty percent of the area of the city was affected, numerous people met their deaths, and the problems of those who survived were enormous. In the city district of Kampung Melayu, one of the numerous urban villages characterized by informal settlement structures, the flooding of the Ciliwung River reached to the third floor of the self-built houses.

We—teachers and students in the Master of Landscape Architecture Program of the National University of Singapore—dedicated several years of intensive urban analysis and design-oriented research work to the Ciliwung River. Our three consecutive, collaborative Design Research Studios (DRS) were embedded in the Landscape Ecology research module of the Future Cities Laboratory (FCL), led by Professor Christoph Girot (ETH Zurich). FCL had been established by ETH Zurich in Singapore.

The first Future Cities Lab, with a total of ten research modules and over 100 researchers, extended over a period of five years (2011–16), and was organized under the auspices of the Singapore-ETH Centre for Global Environmental Sustainability (SEC). The project was financed by means of research funding from the National Research Foundation Singapore (NRF). The *draußen—out there* exhibition in Munich includes impressions and results of the Design Research Studios mentioned, in which two cohorts of students in the Master of Landscape Architecture Program of the National University of Singapore (NUS MLA) were involved. The works relate to the Ciliwung River in the area of the informal settlements of Kampung Melayu, Kampung Bukit Duri, and Kampung Pulo, which are located in the central area of the city of Jakarta.

◀

Location of the specific area of study on the Ciliwung River in Jakarta, Indonesia

When we stood on the bank of the Ciliwung in Jakarta for the first time, it was dry season. The river seemed harmless and sluggish, but the signs in its surroundings spoke another language. Rubbish and refuse not only towered meter-high along the earth of the riverbank, it also hung at absurd heights in the trees and could be interpreted as an ominous harbinger of the next temperamental outbreak of the tropical river, whose tame appearance was only temporary. The Ciliwung has degenerated into a wastewater trench that overflows seasonally. As sad as this might seem, it only visualizes the horrifying state of Jakarta's environment as a whole. The commitment of hundreds of thousands of neighbors of the river— those people who live in the informal settlements along the rivers of the megacity—to largely dispose of all of their garbage directly in the waterways, may not belie the incredible but true fact that Jakarta as a whole has nearly no functioning wastewater system. Affected by this truly only barely comprehensible circumstance are not only residents of slums, but also the elegant guests sitting on the gilded toilet seats at five-star hotels in Jakarta. They should also know that their excrement will in all likelihood not end up in a municipal wastewater treatment plant, but instead in the local soil, groundwater, river, or sea. This is how the urban reality found around the globe in the megacity league of developing and emerging nations looks. We would be outright naïve if we were to classify this as surprising, shocking, disgusting, or the like. Our approach as researching landscape architects and urban planners is to soberly grasp this kind of harsh reality as a research and design challenge.

Rigorous rethinking and openness for changes of mind are among the prerequisites for successful work within an international context. The Western norm is not necessarily helpful everywhere, since such large and problematic cities—such as Jakarta, for example—largely do not exist in the Western context. During our intensive work in the field, along the Ciliwung River, with time, we stopped speaking of "floods," and instead began to understand the "temperament" and the "rhythm" of this natural landscape element. Silently marveling at the imperturbability and optimism of the local population, we began to regard the changing river water levels no longer as a problem, but instead as a prerequisite for a creative rethinking. Rivers and their intermittent flood events are natural phenomena that also have to be put up with in the urban context. One of the most significant characteristics of large-scale urbanized landscapes—around the world—consists of the fact that, despite being built over, the natural processes of these landscapes—just as those of the people who settle in them—will never completely disappear. In spite of all the potential for conflict: the landscape continues to exist, just like the city. One of the parameters that links the two sides of the coin is topography. Both the seasonal fluctuations of the water level of the Ciliwung River and every urban planning

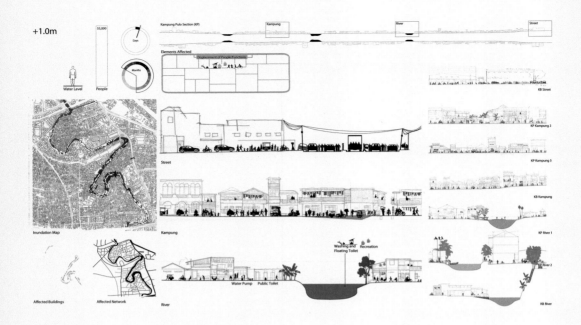

+1.0m

55,000

7
Days

Months

Water Level   People

Inundation Map

Affected Buildings   Affected Network

Kampung Pulo Section (KP)   Kampung   River   Street

Elements Affected   Displacement of People/Functions

KB Street

KP Kampung 2

Street   KP Kampung 3

KB Kampung

Kampung   KP River 1

Washing and   Recreation
Floating Toilet   KB River 2

Water Pump   Public Toilet
River   KB River

▲
Change in the water
level of the Ciliwung
River and temporary
migration in Kampung
Bukit Duri, Jakarta,
due to flooding. The
graphic shows a water
level of one meter
above the normal
level (+ 1.0 m).

intervention along its course are dependent on the local topography. One expression of our in-depth analysis and our detailed understanding of the terrain are precise cross-sections and three-dimensional models. We obtain the corresponding data on site in time-consuming handwork and using the sweat-inducing pedestrian method. In this context, we also experiment with diverse mobile technology. Even in the chaotic megacity, precision still plays an important role. In Jakarta, decimeters and centimeters decide whether the respective abode will be flooded regularly or whether feet will remain dry. Rising water levels—during flood events—force all those who have settled in the, more broadly understood, bed of the rivers to bundle together their belongings and temporarily seek higher floors or higher-lying areas. When the water subsides, people immediately pack their things again and return to where they came from—to the riverbeds. In an urban area situated in a low-lying and steadily sinking delta landscape of thirteen rivers, people have to reckon with the fact that the entire area of the city temporarily mutates into potential riverbeds.

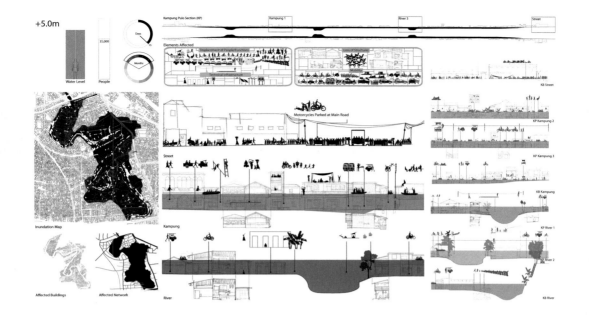

+5.0m

Water Level   People

Days

Months

Kampung Pulo Section (KP)
Kampung 1
River 3
Street

Elements Affected

Displacement of People/Functions   Loss of Structure

Technical Infrastructure

KB Street

KP Kampung 2

Motorcycles Parked at Main Road

KP Kampung 3

Street

KB Kampung

Kampung

KP River 1

KP River 2

River

KB River

Inundation Map

Affected Buildings   Affected Network

▲

Change in the water
level of the Ciliwung
River and temporary
migration in Kampung
Bukit Duri, Jakarta,
due to flooding. The
graphic shows a water
level of five meters
above the normal
level (+ 5.0 m).

Is it then possible to "design" in the usual
manner in such an environment, or does one have no choice other
than to give in to defeatism and the forces of nature? As a group, we
worked very intensively to find an answer to this question. It was first
during the third Design Research Studio—after numerous ambitious
design proposals and approaches—that we painfully owned up to the
fact that we had indeed still not found the right "door" to a truly con-
vincing and satisfactory design strategy. Faced with an endless number of unsolved problems, a central question emerged: "What key
aspect must designers primarily address when attempting to improve
the situation of a place such as the area we were examining?"

Asking ourselves this question and adher-
ing to this motive, we were then in the position to jettison a huge
number of unimportant and clichéd things. In the meantime, we had
measured and come to understand the topography in detail, we were
familiar with the urban building blocks, and it was slowly becoming
clear to us that it was not the river—riverbank, bed, cross-section,
et cetera—that should be changed, but rather the urban layer positioned on top of the river landscape that should be influenced in a decisive way. Our intellectual process was, so to speak, given a helping
hand by the unstoppable forces of nature. While we were wasting
valuable time at an ineffective workshop in Bangkok—the topic was
urban flooding problems although it was dry season in Thailand—
we heard on the news that Jakarta was being hit by the next record

A student in the Master of Landscape Architecture program at the National University of Singapore during the flooding in Jakarta in January 2013

flood. Our students immediately decided to book tickets and fly to the disaster area. This decision marked an important turning point in the course of our studio. Having arrived in Jakarta, all of the partial aspects that had been elaborated up to that point joined together to provide an overall picture, and what was truly at stake became unmistakably clear to the students. All of their previous measuring and drawing work became clear and confirmed by the reality in every dimension. Our studio bore the programmatic title "City in the River," and we now saw the megacity in the middle of the flood with our own eyes. There could no longer be any doubt that it was the topography and the water levels of the rivers that had to serve as irrefutable benchmarks for any design-related intervention on site. Every modified or newly proposed design element had to be water-resistant and waterproof if it was not positioned beyond the maximum possible water level. No single measure made sense if it did not take into account the unalterable flooding and/or river parameters.

The regular floods serve as a natural yardstick; we refer to it as a "horizontal urban trim line," 2013

The future city can only be designed through incorporating knowledge about the natural dynamic. The water levels measured are the yardstick to which everything has to be subordinated; we baptized it the "Horizontal Urban Trim Line." This natural yardstick forces those designing to design everything that lies below it carefully, since this is the urban space that will be beset by masses of water on a regular basis and in perpetuity. Everything that lies above the natural yardstick is less essential, for the most part interchangeable, and comparatively unimportant—from an urbanist perspective. It is not possible for human beings to stop global climate change, and the end of the age of non-sustainable engineering solutions has long since been rung in. Not by internationalist landscape architects, but by the economists of this world.

The "horizontal urban trim line" forces planners to carefully design what lies below it, since this is the area of the city that is regularly and will be affected for eternity by masses of water.

WHATEVER

HORIZONTAL URBAN TRIM LINE

ESSENTIAL

Project data

Project title
City in a River (Jakarta
Studios 2012–13, head:
Jörg Rekittke)

Project team
Prof. Christoph Girot, Prof.
Dr. Jörg Rekittke, Philip Paar,
Yazid Ninsalam, Alexandre
Kapellos, Ilmar Hurkxken,
Magdalena Kaufmann

**Contracting authority/
Funding body**
The Studios were embedded
in the Landscape Ecology
research model led by Pro-
fessor Christoph Girot (ETH
Zurich) of the Future Cities
Laboratory (FCL) established
in Singapore, a project of the
Singapore-ETH Centre. Fi-
nanced with funding from the
Singapore National Research
Foundation

Cooperation partners
Future Cities Laboratory
(FCL), Singapore-ETH
Centre; Chair of Landscape
Architecture, ETH Zurich;
Master of Landscape Archi-
tecture Program, Department
of Architecture, School of
Design and Environment, Na-
tional University of Singapore

Students

**Design Research Studio 01
(2012), National University of
Singapore**
Gauri Barihoke, Guo
Yunjia Lehana, Hou Suya,
Lin Shengwei Ervine,
Muhammad Yazid Ninsalam,
Neha Mehta, Nur Syafiqah
Nahadi, Nur Syuhada Limat,
Sng En Ai Rebecca, Soh Han
Jie, Teo Hui Yi Rachel

**Design Research Studios 02
and 03 (2012/13), National
University of Singapore**
Anna Yap Lai Fong, Fu
Maoying, Heng Juit, Lian,
Pham Le Anh, Ronnie Mak,
Shamy Vivek Darne, Wong
Ruen Qing, Yeo Jiahao,
Zhang Rong

Duration
01/2012–08/2013

Sarah Westropp

Bhinneka Tungall Ika

Bhinneka Tungall Ika, meaning "Unity in Diversity," has been Indonesia's national motto since the end of World War II. With over thirteen thousand islands and thirty-four provinces, it isn't hard to understand why Indonesia is so diverse. This makes it a truly magical place to visit and live. However, it is also the reason conducting business here is so difficult.

For example, I live in Manado, a region in North Sulawesi. Manado and Sulawesi are not only geographically far from the nation's capital; they are also culturally distant. However, even within North Sulawesi, there are huge differences in culture and attitude. In Gorontalo, just south of Manado, there was a recent sighting of whale sharks in their waters. The response from their community has been staggering. From established protection zones to limits on the amount of scuba divers allowed in these areas, the local government and the community were quick to react and eager to get involved in the process.

In contrast, this would never happen in Manado. I think this primarily has to do with cultural differences, especially in regards to attitudes towards authority and power. For the Manadonese, there is less respect for authority because everyone thinks they are the boss. Even though Gorontalo is located in the same region in Indonesia, they don't share this attitude. Even I find it confusing to understand, and I'm a local.

On top of the plethora of cultures and the attitudes that come with them, there are so many varying levels of government—from national to local and everything in between, everyone is on top of each other trying to make and enforce new regulations. Maybe religion is a factor, maybe culture, maybe dialect—how can we enforce just one? Introducing policies that somehow reflect each of these factors is inherently difficult, but especially in a country like Indonesia. An issue specifically affecting my business is the lack of attention the government at a national level places on the Bunaken Marine National Park. While the Indonesian government has some great initiatives to increase levels of marine protection in conjunction with marine tourism, the emphasis is on creating new national parks and enforcing new rules in new areas. There is an assumption that everything is fine in Bunaken because it already has protected status, but this is not the case.

Bunaken can be flooded with rubbish—the pollution can be astounding for a supposed "protected" marine park. The majority of it appears to be variations of plastic items such as water bottles, manufactured by Danone, who definitely don't seem interested in helping to clean up this mess in the long term. This is extremely detrimental not only to the water but to the multitude of organisms that inhabit these waters. Despite the myriad of problems that exist, at the heart of it, I think the number one issue here is the lack of education. I believe that with an emphasis in improving standard education levels across the country, in the long term, the focus on the environment will increase across all Indonesia. Sure, there is no one size fits all policy for sustainable tourism or local governance, but education is the one thing that can at least minimize the gap between these two entities.

∙

Antje Stokman

Changde

Changde, China
                    Sponge City in the Making

            The city of Changde, a typical thriving mid-sized
city of modern China, is a water city. It is located in the western plain
of Lake Dongting on the shore of Yuan River, which is one of the four
major tributaries of the Yangtse River in Southern China. Its surrounding
territory is crisscrossed by hundreds of small rivers, lakes, and wetlands.
The urban-agricultural network of small-scale canals, ditches, and
reservoirs feeds the terraced rice-paddies and provides enough irrigation for two crops of rice a year. Water buffalo and white herons, being
the most common domestic and wild animals adapted to the life in wet
landscapes, are extensively present within the water landscape. Indige-
nous techniques of making the best use of extensive water resources
have evolved from intimate association with climatic, topographic, and
hydraulic conditions and create a productive water-based landscape.

◄   An urban landscape shaped by water along the Chuanzi
     River after the implementation of the project, 2016

Changde's Contested
Water Territories

However, within the fast urban growth of Changde, its connection with water was threatened to become lost: All rivers and water flowing within and around the densely built-up city were engineered to stay outside, pass around, and under it, rather than through it. The quayside road along Yuan River is blocked by a green concrete dike, leaving only a narrow strip of waterfront park along the river. Most of the historic canals, that used to crisscross the city, were filled in and became part of the underground sewage system. The Chuanzi River north of the historic center was cut off from its natural inflow, which was instead directed around the city, and turned into a stagnating water body. Enormous pumps dispose the disposed rainwater from the Chuanzi back into the surrounding river system, consuming a huge amount of energy. This situation resulted in severe problems of water level fluctuation and flooding as well as water pollution, caused by the overflow from seventeen combined rainwater retention and sewage basins that are located along the river. Furthermore these concrete basins are situated adjacent to public and private open spaces, causing danger and stench.

This contrast between the ideal and contested waterscape territory of Changde is a visible metaphor for the actual difficult relationship between humans and nature—and represents a typical situation for many of today's Chinese cities. Taking into account China's socio-hydrological conditions and contemporary urban development challenges, how can Changde's identity be reconstructed based on a hydro-ecological approach to urban landscape?

Changde:
Dry-scape city within
water-scape territory,
2016
▼

Historic Paradigm of Water-Adaptive Chinese Landscapes and Cities

To understand the specific Chinese relationship between water management, territorial planning, and landscape design, one has to take a closer look at China's general water situation and its long tradition of manipulating water for survival. The distribution of water in China is highly unbalanced—both geographically and seasonally. This results in frequent occurrences of drought, flood, and water logging hazards, hence unstable agricultural production, unsafe urban construction, and serious imbalance between water supply and demand.

Due to these unfavorable conditions, the origins of Chinese civilization since more than 3,000 years are closely linked to the state-controlled regulation of water. Going back to Xia Dynasty (21–17 BC) the prominent position of Emperor Da Yu as a controller of water shows the early integration of water control with national leadership. Chinese cultural landscapes are organized and structured by diverse, complex, community-organized systems of water management, which are dependent on large-scale government-managed works of irrigation and flood control. At the same time, hydraulic engineering used to be a major component of urban planning and water infrastructure systems were extremely prominent in most Chinese cities—gaining even more importance as a structural and visual component of urban and regional form than in cultural landscapes dominated by agricultural land use.

Different strategies of combining flood protection and water retention created different types of water-adaptive cities and could create synergies with other important urban functions, such as providing transportation routes for goods and building materials, serving as an open space network for social needs,

▲ Close relationship between historical Chinese cities and water, 2006

▲ Disconnection between city and water because of concreted dikes and river banks

▲ Historic and actual relationship between Changde's urban structure and water management, 2008

supplying water for domestic and industrial uses as well as serving as a system for storm water retention, irrigation, food production, and waste water disposal. Many of the few still existing examples of such kinds of water cities in China have become popular tourist sites— clearly showing that the most profoundly moving urban water landscapes are nothing more than the irrigation, domestic water supply, transportation, sanitary sewer and flood control systems of the time. These urban landscapes allow the site-specific natural processes to be revealed and utilized within the urban fabric and create a specific identity of each city.

Fiascoes of Modern Urban
Development in China

Until the eighteenth century, China was far advanced in the field of comprehensive, small and large-scale, environmental and hydraulic engineering and landscape transformation. However, entering the phase of fast industrialization and urbanization in the twentieth century, China lost track to transform its historical tradition of incorporating watershed logics with its modern urban development patterns. The communist regime's campaign of the "Great Leap Forward" (1958–61) promoted a philosophy of conquest in defiance of nature and put a sudden end to the long tradition of water-adaptive strategies that evolved in China's long history of survival under hazardous conditions. Due to a strong belief in modern technologies in order to overcome natural restrictions and the rejection of traditional site-adapted strategies, water in modern China is being manipulated on a gigantic scale with a huge impact on the natural hydrological regime: The national government has engaged in a vast scale of hydro-engineering projects, such as the construction of more than 87,000 dams since 1978 and the implementation of the South-North Water Transfer Project to transport water from the southern Yangtze River Basin to China's dry north over more than 1,000 kilometers.

▼　Master plan of the "Water City Changde" by Wasser Hannover, 2009

However, at the same time, the number of Chinese cities affected by floods, extreme droughts, and severe water pollution is heavily increasing. Along with the rapid urbanization and extreme urban growth, sealed surfaces and uncontrolled wastewater disposal have increased—and still continue to do so—at mind-boggling speed. Beyond, the ongoing growth of urban population faces a very limited area suitable for construction and as a result more and more people settle in areas that are threatened by floods. With the rivers becoming a major threat to urbanization, most of them have been transformed into concrete channels. A vast network of underground water pipes, pumps, and sewer systems has replaced open watercourses, which are neither visible nor accessible. Modern Chinese culture is treating water as an enemy that can only be overcome by increasingly aggressive interventions. Based on the assumption of water problems being solved by engineers in a technical way, the urban and landscape designers limit themselves to aesthetic and spatial design issues of urban water landscapes—without any consideration of the availability and quality of water, increasing the pressures on the natural hydrological regime even more. In the twentieth century, the urban structure of cities has become increasingly dissociated from the organization of the hydraulic system, erasing the visual and spatial logic of the urban watershed. How to overcome this paradigm by redefining the relationship between water and cities in the twenty-first century?

▼   Schematic diagram of the Sponge City approach, 2009

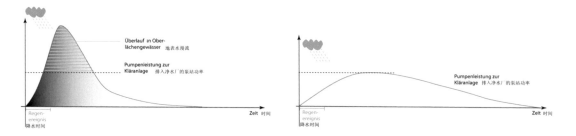

Changde Becoming a
Pioneer "Sponge City"

Since the year 2013, the Chinese national government has started to introduce a new framework for integrated urban water management and design called the "Sponge City" approach. "A sponge city is one that can infiltrate, clean, purify and drain water in a natural way using an ecological approach," says Professor Kongjian Yu, who has supported the initiation of this national project. In 2015, the Chinese government launched an initiative of selecting and supporting sixteen model "sponge cities," which will receive around $63 million per year for three years to implement projects—with Changde being the smallest one out of the selected model cities.

Changde's success to be nationally acknowledged and supported in its transformation towards as a "Sponge City" had its origins in international cooperation and academic inquiry between expert teams from Hannover, Germany, and Changde, China. Combined research studies, study visits to see successful projects in Europe, and professional exchange and student projects developed within the framework of an EU Asia Pro Eco project on integrated water management from 2005–08 served as a seed for the process of transformation, which was supported by the initiation of a deep political commitment and friendship between the two municipalities of Changde and Hannover. Seeing the potential in the results of initial academic studies, in 2008 the City of Changde and Hunan Province commissioned an interdisciplinary group of firms and academics from Wasser Hannover to develop a Framework Master Plan (2007–2020) on Sustainable and Ecological Water Resource Management in the City of Changde as a model project.

Water treatment park
with constructed
wetland alongside
Chuanzi river under
construction, 2010
▼

This plan proposed concrete guidelines and projects to create an urban water landscape with a clear connection between the underlying structure of hydrology and water engineering as the major structuring foundation of urban form, such as the use of catchments as the basis for physical planning and regulation. At the same time it proposed to make use of the obvious synergies between the need to create networks of open space to serve social and ecological needs within the growing city and low-tech, ecological approaches to engineering and urban water management. This means that the different elements of water infrastructure no longer relate only to their own networks defined merely by functionality and efficiency but to their context of cultural, social and ecological processes within the urban matrix: shifting towards more integrated hybrid typologies of infrastructure becoming landscape and landscape becomes infrastructure.

Water treatment park with constructed wetland alongside Chuanzi river after implementation, 2016

Transformation of
Changde's Waterscapes
through Pilot Projects

Building up on the framework master plan, a series of pilot projects were implemented by Wasser Hannover throughout the city of Changde, demonstrating how flood protection, drainage, and water purification systems as a hybrid of built infrastructure, ecological functions and people's green space can serve as fundamental components of changing the urban landscape. The upgrading of several wastewater basins along the Chuanzi River demonstrates how to combine the low-cost improvement of its technical performance with affordable measures to improve the design and ecology of the waterfront park. Technically, the basin is subdivided into several chambers to assure that the water gets treated in different ways, according to the quantity and quality of the water. After a first pre-treatment, the mixed overflow (storm and sewer water) from the water basins is cleaned in a series of constructed wetlands and becomes an essential part of the riverpark's landscape design.

Embedded into a riparian waterfront design with multifunctional flood zones and levees, the upgrading of the waste water basins serves as a starting point for the design of new public water landscapes by an interdisciplinary team of water engineers and landscape architects. Making use of dynamic and self-correcting natural processes, the new seventy-hectare river park performs as an "artificial ecology" that contains a higher degree of ecological resilience, requires little intervention and technical control while, at the same time, offering attractive landscape experiences and creating a high urban biodiversity. It invites people to spend their time nearby the water and offers enough space for a large variety of urban functions, such as promenades, jogging paths, fitness stations, sports grounds, cafés, and a natural swimming pool. As an expression of cooperation and friendship, the city of Changde built its own "Hannover district," including German shops and coffee houses, right on the shore of the Chuanzi River, which was jointly opened by the two mayors in October 2016.

◀ New urban landscape along the Chuanzi river at night after the implementation of the project, 2016

A Landscape Approach
to Designing Water
Cities of the Future

One of the key problems of current global
urbanization trends, as illustrated by the case of Changde, is related
to the deficiencies of conventional engineering concepts of urban
drainage and purification systems—and a lot of money is going to be
invested into exploring new solutions in the future. Rather than leaving this field only to engineers, the discipline of Landscape Architecture should use this window of opportunity to take a leading part in
the reconstruction and development of urban infrastructure systems,
taking the landscape as a starting point. The transformation process
of many cities in China to become "Sponge Cities" provides a strategic chance to strengthen the cooperation between civil engineers,
ecologists, urban designers, and landscape architects to implement
new integrated solutions. By reuniting the engineered and the natural,

Chinese "Sponge Cities" might lead the way towards more resilient hydro-ecological landscapes as a base of sustainable urban and regional form in the twenty-first century. To learn from China, both from its ancient traditions, current challenges, and actual strategies, can reclaim the territory of water infrastructure back into significant urban and landscape design.

Project data

Project title
Sponge City, Changde, China

Project team
Prof. Antje Stokman, Susanne Zeller, Christoph Wust, Yingying Zhu (Leibniz Universität Hannover, Institute of Open Space Development and Planning), Dr. Lothar Fuchs, Chiyan Peng, Dr. Frank Schneider (ITWH Institute for Technical and Scientific Hydrology (limited company)), Carsten Rindfleisch, Andreas Tangen (agwa GmbH), Dr. Holger Pabsch, Olaf Georgi, Jan-Willm Boochs (ipp Pabsch & Partner mbH), Uwe Klaus (Aquaplaner), Prof. Dr. Heinz-Dieter Olbrisch (Ostfalia University of Applied Sciences, Suderburg), Dr. Reinhard Martinsen, Horst Menze (City of Hannover), Rainer Joop (Wasser Hannover e.V.), Axel Hermening, Luc Monsigny, Stefanie Ruff (Levin Monsigny Landscape Architects)

Contracting authority/ Funding body
EU Asia Pro Eco Program, City of Changde, Chuanzi He Investment and Development Association, Hunan Province

Cooperation partners
Wasser Hannover e. V., Stadtentwässerung Hannover, Urban Planning Authority of the City of Changde (China), City of Utrecht (the Netherlands)

Projects and follow-up projects
Sustainable Problem Solutions for Asian Urban Settlements and Developments by Exemplary Analysis of Sewage and Waters of the Urban Settlement Changde and its Chuanzi River Basin, China (12/2005–07/2008); Framework Master Plan on Sustainable and Ecological Water Resource Management in the City of Changde (01/2008–11/2008); Ecological River Rehabilitation Jiangbei, Changde—Part ChuanMaTou (10/2010–05/2012, ARGE Water Quality Improvement Chuanzi)

Students
Project work in the summer semester in 2006: Linlin Du, Markus Klemmer, Bin Lu, Nengshi Zheng, Can Chen, Tanja Kemski, Anna Martens, Yingying Zhu

Degree theses
Yingying Zhu, Nengshi Zheng

Duration
12/2005–today

Acknowledgments
This article and exhibition is based on a large number of interconnected projects by Wasser Hannover that involved many different academics, students, and professionals from different disciplines, both from China and Germany from 2005 until now. It would not have been possible without the endless efforts and high personal engagement of Mr. Chiyan Peng from ITWH Institut für technisch-wissenschaftliche Hydrologie GmbH, who originates from Changde and has lived and worked in Hannover for many years—he built the link for exchanging knowledge and expertise from both cultural contexts. The successful cooperation also would not have been possible without the outstanding support and friendship between the municipalities of Changde and Hannover that was initiated and grew throughout the project.

Kongjian Yu, Dihua Li

The Dream of Sponge Cities Is Starting to Become True

China is facing two main interrelated problems when it comes to water. On the one hand, the country has major problems with urban flooding. China's high-speed urbanization causes a vast increase of sealed areas and rainwater runoff. When being released into sewers and rivers this creates increasing problems: Since 2008, the number of Chinese cities affected by floods has more than doubled. And of China's 657 cities, nearly half fail to meet national standards for flood prevention. On the other hand, China's growing cities have an enormous need for fresh water. Due to overuse and effects of climate change, severe and extreme droughts have become more serious since the late 1990s—half of China's cities are considered water scarce or severely water scarce by UN measures. Chronic water shortages in northern China have led to the construction of a $81 billion canal to transfer water south to north.

As response to these enormous water challenges, through our work at Peking University and Turenscape, we formed the theory of "Sponge City." A sponge city is one that can hold, clean, and drain water in a natural way using an ecological approach. After pouring more than enough concrete to build "gray" infrastructure, now time has come to do major investments in a new type of "ecological" infrastructure. Based on the theory of ecosystem services and landscape security patterns, the "Sponge City" approach is built upon multi-scale hydro-ecological infrastructure to provide an integrated solution to the prominent water problems in urban and rural areas of China. Reverse-engineering a city to make it more spongey requires even more a mental than physical shift, a whole new philosophy of dealing with water in an ecological way. This also requires finding suitable solutions for every specific situation, relating to the local soils, climate, biodiversity and culture.

▲ Qunli National Wetland Park in Harbin (Turenscape, Beijing), 2015

In the past two decades, through practical projects, we developed and tested the sponge city approach in many large-scale pilot cases, like the Qunli National Wetland Park in Harbin implemented in 2011, as a reference. This is a thirty-four hectares new park right in the middle of Qunli New Town, which is listed as a protected regional wetland. Through our design, we managed not only to preserve the threatened wetland, but to transform the area into an urban storm water park that collects, cleanses and stores storm water, infiltrates it into the aquifer, protects and recovers the native habitats, provides a public space for recreational use and aesthetics experience, as well as fostering urban development. This project demonstrated that it is feasible to preserve and design an urban wetland in the middle of a city to provide multiple ecosystems with a relatively small investment by working with nature rather than against it. As a result, the storm water park has not only become a popular urban amenity for the citizens of Qunli New Town, but has also been upgraded to a National Urban Wetland Park because of its improvement to ecological and biological conditions.

Our sponge city concept goes far beyond the LID scope to include flood adaptive solutions. The project of Yanweizhou in Jinhua City, built in 2014, is one of a series of demonstration projects. Due to its monsoon climate, Jinhua suffers from annual flooding. Hard high walls were supposed to be built to protect the last existing patch of riparian wetland. These floodwalls would have created dry parkland above the water while destroying the lush and dynamic wetland ecosystem. Therefore, we devised a contrasting solution: We managed to convince the city authority to stop the construction of the concrete floodwall and to demolish others. Instead, the Yanweizhou project "makes friends" with flooding by using a cut-and-fill strategy to balance earthwork by creating a water-resilient terraced river embankment that is covered with flood adapted native vegetation. Floodable pedestrian paths and pavilions are integrated with the planting terraces, which will be closed to the public during the short period of flooding. The floods bring fertile silt that is deposited over the terraces and enrich the growing condition for the tall grasses that are native to the riparian habitat. The terraced embankment will also remediate and filtrate the storm water from the pavement above.

Based on many years of research and practice, several proposals were sent to the top leaders of the Chinese government calling for the action of an ecological approach and sponge city practice on a national scale. Our efforts were also combined with other international and national leaders in this field, including the international expert group advising the city of Changde since 2005. Public awareness was further strengthened by the increasing urban inundation problems that Chinese were facing, particularly the 2012 flood in the capital city Beijing, that caused the death of seventy-nine people, with some of them losing their lives on the streets and in their cars.

Finally, at China's Central Government Conference on Urbanization in 2013, the Chinese President Xi Jinping promoted the concept by announcing that cities should act "like sponges."

▲   Yanweizhou in Jinhua City (Turenscape, Beijing), 2015

To support this national initiative, in 2015 the national government offered a substantial amount of funding for sixteen pilot cities (including the city of Changde, being the smallest out of the selected cities), which are receiving up to $63 million per year over three years for water-related initiatives. An additional fourteen cities were added in 2016. While before 2013 nobody knew the term "sponge city," meanwhile city leaders all over China have taken up the concept. In 2016, China's State Council announced a new set of urbanization guidelines stating that all new urban developments should have sponge city-like water-retention capabilities, essentially making this strategy a new national standard. Of course, only to do a pilot park or pilot neighborhood is not enough— for the sponge city approach to really make a difference the existing gray infrastructure of cities including sewer systems and flood protection measures need to be gradually retrofitted on a large scale. With the innovations gradually scaling up, China is likely to become a pioneer in the large-scale application of the "sponge city" concept and serve as a model for cities throughout the globe.

Antje Stokman

Lima

Lima, Peru
City without Water

   The Peruvian capital of Metropolitan Lima is located on a desert coast overlooking the Pacific Ocean. With its more than 9.5 million inhabitants, Lima is considered the most extensive desert city in the world after Cairo. It has an average of only nine millimetres of rainfall per year. The glaciers feeding its three main rivers are melting and the groundwater table has already reached critical levels. Therefore, Lima is considered as one of the most vulnerable megacities in the world to the effects of climate change. At the same time, Lima is facing a vast expansion of its informal settlements. They consume land with important ecosystem functions such as mist-fed mountain habitats, coastal wetlands, and river floodplains as well as fertile agricultural valleys, and leave a large proportion of the population in risky and vulnerable living conditions. At the same time, they lack many basic urban services including water supply and wastewater infrastructure, which has caused severe sanitary problems as well as environmental degradation. Around twenty percent of Lima's population, mainly living in the hilly and peri-urban areas, do not have access to the public water supply or wastewater services. They receive drinking water, often of very bad quality, from private water vendors at high prices.

◀ Lima, city in the desert: aerial view of informal settlements encrouching the foothills of the Andes Mountains in Lima, 2012

Challenges of Lima's
Urban Water Cycle

In order for urban vegetation to survive in a desert environment, vegetated parks, gardens, and road greenery in Lima need to be irrigated. Due to Lima's water scarcity and urban segregation, in many dusty peri-urban areas there are less than two square meters of green area per person while richer areas have more than twenty square meters of green area per person. Overall, Lima is one of the Latin American cities with the amount of least green area per inhabitant. The majority of urban green areas are designed in a decorative manner, based on water-intensive lawns and artificial ponds, with little consideration of the desert environment. This results in a very high water demand, which is even increased by the inhabitants' lack of awareness about water saving and inefficient technologies.

At the same time, the treated wastewater from most wastewater treatment plants in Metropolitan Lima does not meet the standards for the irrigation of green areas. Therefore only a small amount (only ten percent in 2011) of the total treated wastewater is officially reused for irrigation, while the use of drinking water for irrigation purposes puts even more stress on the limited, expensive, and scarce water resources. So far, the treated wastewater is not seen as a resource but discharged into rivers, canals, and the ocean, often with insufficient quality. However due to the high cost and lack of drinking water, in many informal areas untreated wastewater is informally misused for irrigation purposes, with bad hygienic consequences. The agencies responsible for different water-related issues are neither sharing their data nor coordinating their actions. Therefore Lima's hydrological systems as well as its urban landscape need radical rethinking to make engineered and landscape systems perform in concert with one another and keep up with the increasing water demand for a growing, more livable and green city.

◀ Two sides of the mountain, with expensive villas of the rich on the one side and informal settlements of the poor on the other side, seperated by a wall, 2016

▲ Aerial view of informal settlements over steep hills in Ate District, 2013

International
Research Cooperation
Supporting Lima's
Water-Sensitive Future
Urban Development

From 2008 to 2014, the German-Peruvian research project Sustainable Water Management in Urban Growth Centres Coping with Climate Change—Concepts for Metropolitan Lima, Peru (LiWa) initiated dialogues and developed scenarios, tools, technologies, integrated planning strategies, and pilot projects for Lima's water-sensitive future urban development. A new approach combining infrastructure design, landscape and spatial design acts as a catalyst for landscape transformation and assists in developing an alternative water culture for Lima's future.

◀ Loma ecosystem and
informal settlements in
winter (humid season),
2013

The Lima Ecological Infrastructure Strategy
(LEIS) shows different strategies to integrate the water cycle into
a multifunctional open space system, which at the same time is
designed to improve and protect the water cycle and act as a framework for urban development. It stresses the need for adapting
the current urban water management according to the dry context
of a desert city, considering the city both as a "water source"
and a "catchment area." At the same it aims to improve the city's
resilience to cope with climate change by promoting low-tech and
decentralized water purification technologies, reusing non-potable
water for irrigation, catching the fog to produce water, and implementing less water-consuming planting design. Based on satellite
imagery analyses and a geographical information system (GIS) based
tool to understand the city as system of different "hydro-urban units,"
general planning principles and policy recommendations, a design
manual as well as a simple design testing and water demand calcula-
tion tool were developed. The manual shows different water-sensitive
design strategies relating to different urban space typologies in
terms of their urban structure and open space systems (formal and
informal), their geomorphology (slope and soil), and their hydrological
aspects (availability of water sources and the current state of water
infrastructure).

▼ Water trucks providing
drinking water to
informal settlements,
2013

▼ Impression of greening
despite water scarcity
in informal settlement,
2012

Loma ecosystem and
informal settlements in
summer (dry season),
2013

The Lower Chillón
River Watershed as a
Demonstration Area for
Spatial Strategies and
Pilot Projects

  In order to demonstrate water-sensitive
urban development in practice, the lower Chillón River watershed in
the north of Lima and Callao was chosen as a demonstration area.
Here, the Chillón River does not carry any water between May and
December, while becoming a torrent and causing floods in urban
areas in the rest of the year. Several pollutants affect the water quality in different sections of the river, including the discharge of raw
domestic wastewater and industrial wastewater, drainage from agricultural areas with high concentrations of fertilizers, as well as
insufficiently treated effluent from the wastewater treatment plant.
Irrigation channels divert polluted water from the river to irrigate
the remaining agricultural fields in the valley. A highlight within this
area are the valuable cultural heritage sites from pre-Inca times, like
the temple El Paraiso (2000 BC), which are hardly accessible to the
public yet.

  A Strategic Landscape Framework Plan for
the lower Chillón River watershed was developed in order to demonstrate possibilities for a water-sensitive spatial development, that
can serve as a model for the entire watershed through an integrative
approach. This plan integrates water management and landscape
planning with social, cultural, and economic aspects, thus guiding the
implementation of a water-sensitive demonstration area. It suggests
strategic projects, like a public space system along the irrigation channels and a new dike system including constructed wetlands for water
purification as part of the future Chillón River Park whilst improving
the cultural landscape and archaeological heritage. In parallel, additional strategic concepts for other sites were developed through final
thesis projects, e.g., the Loma Park proposal for catching fog on the
hillsides. The River Park project was developed in detail and accepted
by the municipal administration Services for Parks in Lima (SERPAR),
which allocated a budget for its construction. This project is currently
in the process of technical and legal resolution. All plans and projects
were presented to the local planning authorities of Metropolitan
Lima with the aim to be considered in actual planning projects such
as the Land Management Plan and the Urban Development Plan for
Metropolitan Lima.

Construction of water sensitive urban design prototypes during summer school, 2012

Participatory workshop to co-design Parque de los Niños in Chuquitanta, 2012

Monitoring of constructed wetland within Parque de los Niños, 2015

The park developed well over time and is much-used by the children, 2016

Learning by Participatory Design, Experimentation, and Testing of New Solutions

To start the actual implementation of the strategic projects, different prototype solutions were designed and built in an effort to communicate, test, and promote water-sensitive solutions at a smaller scale. These on-site solutions were developed within two interdisciplinary summer schools attended by German and Peruvian architecture and engineering students, as well as agriculture and social science students. By starting the process with a series of minimal temporary installations relating to the different water sources, spaces, and actors within the area, the viability of different concepts was discussed both with experts from different institutions, as well as the local community. Their implementation, opening and the resulting public exhibitions of results in the city center of Lima focused attention on the topics and the necessity of water-sensitive urban development in this zone.

Building up on these experiences, a first pilot project was designed to demonstrate that a park can treat the contaminated water of existing irrigation channels to reuse it for the irrigation of urban green areas, use less water than a conventional park, and at the same time create an attractive public space for the community. The park was implemented in 2014 and is composed of three main parts, including a constructed wetland system with a reservoir for treated wastewater, a green recreational area with fruit trees, and a children's play area with dry surfaces and trees to provide shade. The design phase of the park, following a participatory approach, was used to reestablish a dialogue among neighbors, the center Chuquitanta, and the local authorities. While overall contributing to improve the relationships between the different actors, tensions arose in dealing

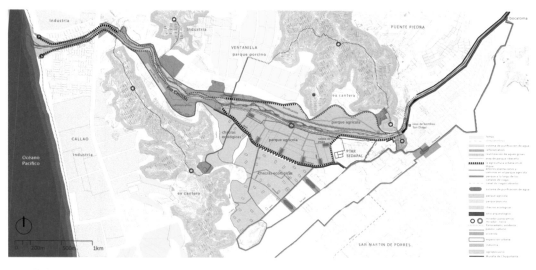

▲ Ecological Infrastructure Framework Plan for Lower Chillón River Watershed, 2013

▼ Parque de los Niños in Chuquitanta on the inauguration day in August, 2014

▼ Design Proposal Parque Lomas, visualization dry season, 2012

▼ Rio Chillón in dry season without water, 2013

▼ Rio Chillón in wet season with flood, 2013

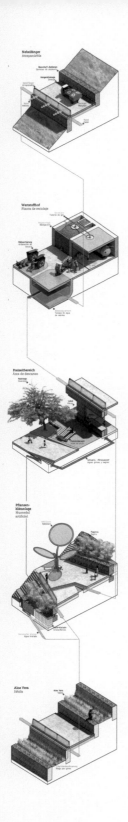

◀

Design features/water
cycle within Parque
Lomas, 2012

with the shared responsibilities and different expectations on the maintenance of the park. Therefore, to build strong partnerships between these stakeholders is critical for the current and future sustainability of the park and its treatment system.

Overall, the project Lima Beyond the Park shifts the focus from the current practice of "image based" open space design to "performance based" open space design. It no longer considers urban open space an expensive luxury but one that needs to save water, purify water, treat wastewater and recycle nutrients or even harvest water.

●

Project data

Project title
Lima Beyond the Park

Project team
Prof. Antje Stokman, Dr. Bernd Eisenberg, Eva Nemcova, Rossana Poblet (Institute of Landscape Planning and Ecology, University of Stuttgart)

Contracting authority/ Funding body
BMBF Future Megacity Program, DAAD, Sto-Stiftung

Project participants
Dr. Manfred Schütze, ifak Magdeburg (overall coordination BMBF-Project LiWa), Dr. Christian D. León, ZIRIUS, University of Stuttgart (coordination in Peru BMBF-Project LiWa), Prof. Dr. Arthur Mennerich, Ingeborg Joost, Henning Schuba (Ostfalia University of Applied Sciences, Faculty of Construction-Water-Soil), Juan Espinola, Luis Jara, Claudia Santisteban (Metropolitan Planning Institute, Lima), Linda Zilbert, Liliana Miranda (NGO FCPV Lima), Julio Moscoso (Lima), Prof. Rosa Miglio (National Agricultural University La Molina, Lima), Prof. Rosa Yaya (National University of Engineering, CITRAR, UNI), Cesar Palomino, Paul Lopez, Rosa Gutierrez, Kia Miranda, Mercedes Romero, Eduardo Zambrano, Carlos Restrepo, Frédérique Jonnard, Merino Reyna Evelyn, AKUT Peru, Milagros Juarez, Rodolfo Navarro (La Florida II), Maribel Zapater-Pereyra (UNESCO-IHE), Marius Ege, Andrea Balestrini, Raoul Humpert, Louis Maldonado, Katherine Polo

Cooperation partners
Metropolitan Planning Institute (IMP, Lima), Juan Reiser (CIAC, Pontificia Catholic University of Peru, Lima), Jochen Beerhalter (Lima), Sedapal (Lima), Serpar (Lima), Luis Alvarado (San Martin de Porres), Centro de Investigación de la Arquitectura y la Ciudad-CIAC (PUCP, Lima), National University of Engineering (UNI, Lima)—Research Centre for Wastewater Treatment and Hazardous Waste (CITRAR Lima), National Agricultural University La Molina (UNALM, Lima)

Students:

Design studio winter semester 2011/12
Christos Antoniou, Andrea Balestrini, Lisa Gänsbauer, Meike Hammer, Sofia Holder, Nefeli Marilena Kaltsouni, Anna Ilonka Kubler, Maximilian Mehlhorn, Silke Mittnacht, Anna Oelrichs, Julian Andreas Winkelhofer, Leonie Wipf, Dessire Velez

Summer university 2012
Xhrstos Antoniou, Andrea Balestrini, Marius Ege, Lisa Gänsbauer, Meike Hammer, Sofia Holder, Nefeli Marilena Kaltsouni, Anna Ilonka Kübler, Maximilian Mehlhorn, Silke Mittnacht, Anna Oelrichs, Julian Winkelhofer, Leonie Wipf, Dessire Velez, Pamela Acuña, Tania Barrenechea, Andrea Pérez Fu, Jonathan Lapel, Ricardo Pacheco, Pablo Pajares, Katherine Polo, Rolando Tafur, Kathya del Pilar Aliaga, Luis Maldonado Cueva, Carolina Espinoza, Danny Paytán Ordoñez, Annie Salvador Rosas, Víctor Huaman Torres, Bruno Arce, Diego Rios, Kara McElhinney

Design studio winter semester 2012/13
Silvana Bay, Benjamin Feller, Karin Hauser, Astrid Paul, Carmen Schwarz, Veronica Schubach, Ines Wulfert, Omar Cuya, Andrea Dominguez, Andrea Ramirez, Jose Ojeda, Cinthya Barros, Lizbeth Fernandez, Jonathan Jaramillo

Summer university 2013
Tjark Bornemann, José Cáceres, Eva Damm, Joselyn Daniel, Benjamin Feller, José Gutierrez, Jonathan Jaramillo, Rosa Paredes, Astrid Paul, Andrea Ramírez, Luis Santos, Carmen Schwarz, Paul Stegmann, Petra Wiesbrock, Jessie Wolters, Ines Wulfert, Juan Carlos Zapata, Alicia Aguinaga, Cynthia Aguirre, Andrea Asman, Silvana Bay, Claudia Coronel, Andrea Dominguez, Karin Hauser, Hawell Huarhuachi, Dimitra Megas, Mirko Mertens, Ana Quinto, Arturo Salazar, Genevieve Sevlo, Diego Suero, Marianne Trauten, Magdalena Wallkamm

Diploma/Master theses 2012–today
Marius Ege, Andrea Ballestrini, Astrid Paul, Bruno Arce

Duration
April 2011–today

Rosa Maria Miglio Toledo De Rodriguez

Lessons from the Children's Park

As Lima is one of the Latin American cities with the largest lack of green areas, there is a strong need to develop innovations how to provide green public spaces, especially for the urban poor. So far, most public and private green areas in Lima are irrigated either with scarce potable water or with polluted surface water, while the reuse of treated wastewater remained as low as 10% in 2011 (Kosow et al. 2013). Therefore, the use of decentralized wastewater treatment technologies and recycling wastewater for the irrigation of green areas should be promoted in a dry megacity, such as Lima. The advantage of the nature-based technology of constructed wetlands is that they generate green areas by themselves and therefore have a high potential to be integrated in open space design in arid areas.

As part of the research project LiWa (Lima Water), a pilot project was designed, built, and tested in order to evaluate the applicability of such a concept in the context of Lima. The main aim of the project was to implement a wastewater treatment park within a peri-urban area without access to the public water supply or wastewater service—representing many of the existing informal settlements with almost one million people in Lima. A constructed wetland as the main design element of the park should treat contaminated water for reuse in the irrigation of green areas, use less water than a conventional park in Lima, and at the same time provide an attractive public space for the community. In a broader scope, the project aims to reflect on the potential of Water Sensitive Urban Design to support cities in dry climatic conditions to prepare and cope with water scarcity and climate change effects.

The pilot project Wastewater Treatment Park–Children's Park is located in the community La Florida II, San Martin de Porres district, in the north of Lima. The informal housing area is in the process of obtaining urban legal rights, which will be received once the real estate company completes the basic infrastructure. The site of the pilot project is situated directly next to a heavily polluted irrigation channel, which was converted into a concrete channel in 2012 to comply with the requirements for obtaining the formalization of La Florida II. The removal of trees and grass alongside the new channel caused a conflict between the community and the municipal authorities, as the community felt that the regularization process acts "against the environment" and caused the disappearance of urban green from their direct environment. Therefore, the pilot project had to involve, try to create synergies, and resolve conflicts between the different stakeholders, including the community representatives, the Agricultural Irrigation Commission and the Municipality of San Martin de Porres. The project team, led by the Institute of Landscape Planning and Ecology of Stuttgart University, followed a participative approach to reestablish a dialogue and a joint vision for the future of the open space system of La Florida II.

Technically, the park comprises three main parts including a constructed wetland system with a reservoir of treated wastewater, a green recreational area with fruit trees for passive recreation, and a play area for active recreation with dry surfaces and trees to provide shade. The constructed wetland is situated at the highest point of the park in order to reduce the need for pumping. The elevated edge of the constructed wetland was designed as a seating bench with a wooden deck and educational panels, informing the community about the water source and quality, treatment process and reuse. The plant species within the constructed wetland contribute significantly to the aesthetic aspect of the treatment system and are key features of the park. Only forty percent of the total park area is planted with grass and native fruit

▲   Lower Chillón River Watershed, Metropolitan Lima

▼   La Florida II settlement with San José irrigation channel and the project area on the left of the channel before construction

▲ Constructed wetland with the seating bench, wood deck and educational panel about the San José water source, "San Pepito droplet"

▼ Green productive recreational area and the dry play area in the foreground

trees. The remaining area consists of dry surfaces with solitary trees of native species (mimosa) and xerophytes. The careful selection of vegetation and the use of pressurized irrigation systems resulted in a low overall water demand for the total area.

After the opening of the Children's Park in August 2014, a survey was conducted in order to evaluate the sustainability of the treatment system and its acceptance by the local inhabitants. The results of the monitoring could prove that the water quality improved drastically, including the reduction of turbidity, BOD5 and fecal coliforms. The treatment system has a positive impact in terms of reducing health risks, smell and the presence of vectors of waterborne diseases. Concerns remain about the presence of insects, which should be further investigated. In social terms, it was perceived by the community, that park development helped to improve relationships between the actors. However, the operation and maintenance by the district administration continues to be a challenge. The municipal workers are not well-trained and too few to take care of all public spaces. Therefore the community does not receive enough support while paying taxes for public services and the maintenance of public space. Overall, the partnership between these stakeholders remains the most critical concern for the current and future sustainability of the park. Also safety issues create some challenges, as the surrounding areas are characterized by crime, alcohol and drug abuse. The height of the wetland plants could provide a hiding space for criminals. An incident of attempted attack was experienced and therefore the community decided to cut down the vegetation to a medium height.

Overall, the results from the project after four years of research and a participatory design process provided important lessons for the more sustainable use of water resources in Lima and specifically in the Lower Chillón River Watershed. It managed to involve communities, metropolitan and local authorities, Peruvian and international students and researchers to demonstrate opportunities for a radical rethinking of public space design, based on saving, purifying and recycling wastewater in an arid city.

Acknowledgment
The project was only possible thanks to great enthusiasm of Eva Nemcova and Rossana Poblet, who coordinated the project from the side of the Institute of Landscape Planning and Ecology of Stuttgart University in cooperation with Cesar Palomino, Paul Lopez and Rosa Gutierrez. The community from La Florida II has shown the power to co-lead the process and support the park design, construction, maintenance and operation. In addition, the German Ministry of Education and Research (BMBF), the San Martin de Porres Municipality, and the community La Florida II co-financed the project with the aim of benefiting the community by gaining a new green space, which can support the reduction of socio-environmental conflicts in the area.

Christian Werthmann

Medellín

9

Medellín, Colombia
Shifting Ground

When it rains for extended periods of time in Medellín, there is a high danger of landslides along the steep slopes of the city. Some 850 people have lost their lives in such incidents in the past one hundred years. The most catastrophic of such landslides swept 500 people to their deaths in the neighborhood of Villatina in 1987. The landslides mainly occur in an area of erosion-prone volcanic soil on the northeastern slopes of the 2.5-million-person metropolis, precisely where the most informal urban growth has taken place over the past fifty years. In Medellín, informal urban growth refers to houses constructed without a building permit on the precariously steep slopes, mostly by low-income persons displaced by the country's prolonged civil war. According to the authorities, around 45,000 of these houses are now located in zones at risk of landslides. The city is planning to resettle the people in subsidized housing, but this is an extremely expensive and protracted undertaking. In addition, a lot of people who live there see things differently. Many feel bullied by the city's resettlement plans and would prefer to remain in their houses.

▸ Resident of the steep slopes of Medellín, 2013

"We come from the mountains. While the city turns its back, the mountains welcome us with open arms."

▸ Refugee from the civil war and a resident of the steep slopes of Medellín, 2013

"If I had stayed where I come from, I would now surely be dead. In my opinion, the landslides are an evil that I am able to live with."

◂ Medellín's new settlers construct their houses on steep slopes at risk of landslides. Path construction and the excavation of escarpments open up the vegetation cover and the risk of landslides increases, 2015

Despite municipal bans on construction, buildings are still rapidly being erected on the dangerous slopes. If one extrapolates the current rate of growth of Medellín as a whole, then approximately 70,000 more people will live on these perilous slopes by 2030. What can be done?

Faced with this situation, the Columbian planning institute Urbam at EAFIT University, under the direction of the architect Alejandro Echeverri, joined forces with the specialist field of landscape architecture and design of Leibniz Universität in Hannover, under my direction, to develop alternative scenarios for Medellín's northeastern slopes on behalf of the municipal government. In an initial regional study (Rehabitar la Ladera, Shifting Ground, 2012), our team, accompanied by a geologist, considered the entire Aburrá Valley in two respects: the history and future of informal growth in Medellín and the location and logic of landslides in this valley.

One important realization was that the designation of absolute limits for construction in Medellín has led to an increase in informal building activities beyond these boundaries—achieving precisely the opposite of what was initially intended. This realization led us to search for strategies that were based not on "hard" prohibitions, but rather on "soft" benefits for the local population.

The second important realization was that the types of landslides on Medellín's slopes vary. In some zones, the landslides are triggered so deep that there is no effective way to prevent them from occurring or to mitigate their damage. The soil becomes saturated with rising ground water along a deep slippage plane leading to total slope failure. In other zones, by contrast, the landslides are much shallower and often triggered by causes exacerbated by humans, such as inadequate drainage or by negative changes in drainage patterns, for instance, due to drainage ditches becoming filled with garbage or poorly constructed streets. It might be possible to live in such zones if the drainage could be managed and controlled.

When we overlaid the geology of the Aburrá Valley with the informal growth patterns anticipated in the study, we arrived at the sobering conclusion that the majority of informal construction which will likely happen in the coming years could also be expected to continue in areas at risk of landslides. There was now pressure to consider not only corrective, but also anticipative strategies.

In an extensive follow-up study, we expanded our interdisciplinary team to include a biologist and a sociologist, with whom we examined two rapidly expanding districts of the city, La Cruz and La Honda, with a combined total of around 4,000 houses with an estimated 16,000 residents. We wanted to get

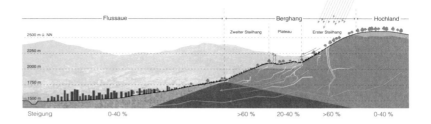

▲ The City of Medellín
and its informal settle-
ments shown in black,
2013

▲ Self-constructed settlements grow independently further
up slopes at risk of landslides, 2014

a more accurate picture of the desires, needs, and activities of these
residents as well as of the physical circumstances on the site. What
became apparent in numerous interviews and community meetings
was that most of the residents were quite aware of the physical risk
of landslides, but in the face of other risks, such as, for instance, the
possible loss of employment opportunities, most residents considered the landslide risk to be of minor concern.

▸ Enfren Gonzales, day
laborer, resident of
the steep slopes of
Medellín, 2015

"I know that my house is endangered by
landslides, but I don't think about it very
much, since I simply have no option to
move anywhere else, whatever the case."

▼ View of Medellín from
La Cruz, 2014

◀ Model: La Honda und La Cruz, 2016

Many of the people interviewed were even proud to live on the slopes, describing themselves as "mountain people," and did not want to move. The older of the two districts, La Cruz, was astonishingly well organized with a Defensa Civil, a kind of volunteer fire department comprised of 500 volunteers, who help each other out in times of crisis.

In keeping with a "soft" approach, our team presented our recommendations to the citizens at the community center. The operating principle was that life-threatening risks should be reduced as much as possible by means of measures that support the community in its right to exist and day-to-day life. New construction in life-threatening locations should be monitored by the community and prevented. Unused or evacuated landslide-endangered areas should be designated with a productive land use so as to deter construction.

The basis for all the strategies was an existing landslide risk map for the individual slopes. Slopes where landslide risk could be mitigated should be secured by bioengineering measures. Future informal growth should be directed to slopes with negligible risk of landslides. Residents on slopes that cannot be stabilized should be protected in the short-term by a well-developed early warning system in connection with the development of a clear and safe evacuation system. In the long term, settlers on slopes that cannot be stabilized will, however, have to be resettled somewhere nearby.

One basic prerequisite was that all of the measures proposed should be inexpensive and achievable with self-built construction, and if possible, also provide the community with additional opportunities for income. Everything also has to be easily replicable. To check the feasibility, methodology, and efficiency of the strategies, our team proposed developing five small pilot projects in strategic areas of the settlement in collaboration with the community. These projects should to be validated and adapted by means of ongoing observation and evaluation of the effects so as to work against a customary top-down approach.

▼ If the settlements continue to grow, the number of inhabitants will double by 2030, 2014

HEUTE

2030

The first project should test an early warning and evacuation system. A grid of ground sensors that send out signals in the case of shifts in the earth is installed on a slope that cannot be stabilized. The evacuation system is comprised of an improvement of footpaths and with the provision of lighting for the district, coupled with an upgrading of public spaces that might serve as assembly points after an alarm is sounded, and of educational institutions that could serve as emergency accommodation in the case of an alarm. Since the ground sensors do not leave very much time for evacuation, an appropriate evacuation procedure has to be developed in cooperation with the Defensa Civil.

In the second project, failure points in the storm water runoff system should be identified in cooperation with the community. The inadequacies in the drainage network could be eliminated by means of specific drainage and bioengineering measures that utilize self-built construction. In Columbia, there are organizations that successfully make use of soil bioengineering with bamboo in rural areas to stabilize slopes and minimize risk. Their techniques could also be adapted to urban situations.

The third project would target unoccupied slopes at immediate risk of future settlement, and would prevent informal settlement by a valorization of areas currently not in use. Agricultural use of areas by associations of interested citizens already takes place in other places in Medellín. Targeted marketing of "Medellín Mountain Products" could provide a possible source of income.

The fourth project would target unsettled slopes in the upper areas of the slope at long-term risk of informal settlement, and would make such areas more secure through soil-stabilizing afforestation. This afforestation could be financed with public funds and create workplaces in the community. A civil organization with activists who regularly plant trees on the slopes (Mas bosques) already exists today. The new forests would provide local recreation for the citizens of Medellín.

Finally, in the fifth project, safe locations would be developed with incentives to encourage incremental residential construction. This means that low-income citizens would be enabled to gradually finish the construction of an unfinished house with their own means. Basic infrastructure such as water, electricity, and access is provided. Resettled citizens or new arrivals should thus be given the opportunity to build safely and inexpensively. Positive experience has already been had with projects of this kind since the nineteen-seventies, under the title Sites-and-Services. The greatest challenge in realizing them is finding affordable land and an urban planning framework that is adapted to the steep slopes.

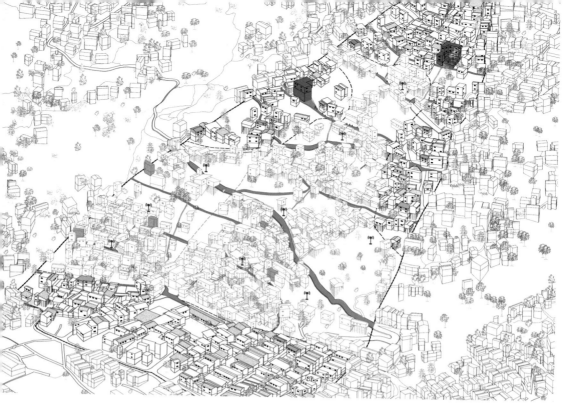

▲   In our first pilot project, we propose a landslide warning
▼   system along with the new construction of an evacuation
     and emergency shelter system, 2016

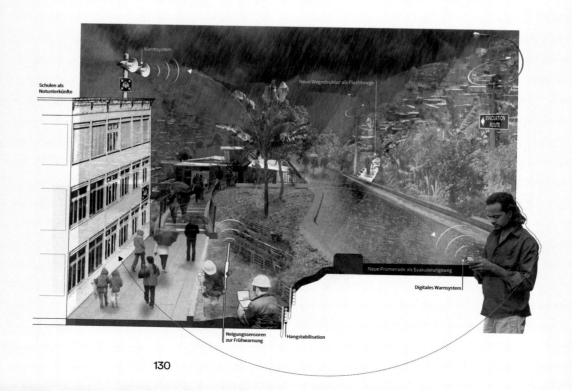

Hangstabilisation

Terassierte
Anbauflächen

Forstwirtschaft

Neues
Wegesystem

Kooperative
Landbewirtschaftung

▲   Hazardous areas that have been cleared of housing can be
     reused for cooperative micro-farming in order to reduce
▼   resettlement risk, 2016

▲ In settlement areas, slopes are supposed to be secured through bioengineering measures and new open spaces be defined, 2016

▲ The not yet settled steep upper slopes are supposed to be secured by means of vegetation-related measures that can be executed by the citizens themselves, 2016

▲ On areas possible for settlement, the construction of houses shall be supported by the provision of basic infrastructure

It is in the first implementation of these proposals on a small scale that the strengths and weaknesses of the proposals can be tested. The optimal goal would be to find an approach for Medellín as a whole that could be translated to other cities with similar problems. According to a database curated at the University of Durham, between 2004 and 2010, there were 2,662 non-seismic landslides worldwide, with a total of 32,322 casualties. Given all the evidence of climate change, with more frequent and stronger rain events, it is anticipated that landslides will occur with increasing frequency around the world. Along with the enduring wave of urbanization in the predominantly poor countries of our planet, more people will be exposed to this risk and correspondingly more deaths will occur. It is therefore urgently necessary to find integrative countermeasures that can be used by citizens directly on site.

Up to this point, the municipal government of Medellín has reacted somewhat hesitantly to our ideas. Our pilot projects have therefore found themselves stuck in the proposal phase since the beginning of 2015. The now-former mayor was more impressed by another, more spectacular project: a magnetic monorail that runs along the steep slopes and links the communities transversely. This infrastructure megaproject was propagated under the guise of a greenbelt. The former leadership of the city regarded our different, gentle form of a greenbelt with its incremental bioengineering measures, mountain farming, afforestation measures, and incremental self-built houses as having too little promotional effectiveness for a modern, up-and-coming city.

The residents of the slopes are naturally hostile to the megaproject. They fear, not completely without justification, that once all the money has been spent on the monorail, there will be none left for them. They also do not see the logic of a transport vehicle that links them with other poor settlements to the left and right, while the paths that they mainly require run not parallel, but instead perpendicular to the slope, namely to the valley floor, to the center of the city, to which the majority of them commute to for work on a daily basis. They also fear, probably rightly so, that such a complex building project will inevitably result in the forced relocation of houses that stand in the way of the project. Among the mountain inhabitants of Medellín, the greenbelt project is thus feared, indeed hated. As of 2016, there is now a new mayor in Medellín, and many of the residents hope that the new municipal government will see the future of the slopes somewhat differently.

Our proposals nevertheless found many open ears and agreement among the citizens of La Cruz and La Honda. They promise them the possibility to remain on the slopes and an improvement in current conditions. Since no assistance is being provided by the city, impatient citizens have meanwhile taken their fate into their own hands. During our last visit in 2015, to our amazement and happy surprise, a young activist told us that we should not worry, since they are currently in the process of making our pilot projects a reality anyway.

Project data

Project title
Medellín, Columbia—
Shifting Ground

Project team
Institute of Landscape Architecture, Leibniz Universität Hannover: Christian Werthmann, Joseph Claghorn, Nicholas Bonard, Florian Depenbrock, Mariam Farhat;

Centro de Estudios Urbanos y Ambientales (urbam)/La Universidad EAFIT (Escuela de Administración, Finanzas e Instituto Tecnológico): Alejandro Echeverri (director), Francesco María Orsini, Juan Sebastian Bustamante Fernández, Ana Elvira Vélez Villa, Isabel Basombrío, Diana Marcela Rincón Buitrago, Juan Pablo Ospina, Anna Manea, Daniela Duque, Ángela Duque, Simón Abad, Lina Rojas, Maya Ward-Karet, Santiago Orbea Cevallos;

Harvard Graduate School of Design: Aisling O'Carroll, Conor O'Shea

Contracting authority
Municipal Planning Authority of the City of Medellín

Cooperation partners
Fundacíon CIPAV, bio-engineering, Fundación Sumapaz, community organization, Aníbal Gaviria Correa, Jorge Pérez Jaramillo, Juan Manuel Patiño M., Paola Andrea López P., Sergio Mario Jaramillo V., David Emilio Restrepo C., Mario Flores, John Cuartas, María Alejandra Rodríguez N.

Participating project specialists
Eva Hacker, soil bioengineering, Marco Gamboa, geology, Michel Hermelin, geology, Iván Rendon, sociology, Tatiana Zuluaga, urban planning

Students in the masters program project (Re)Making Medellín in 2012–13
Carmen Aránzazu Ceron Herrera, Florian Depenbrock, Mariam Farhat, Timo Fritz, Roman Früh, Lena Hörtemöller, David Kreis, Jonas Schäfer, Marc Steindorff Martí, Silvia Terron Panadero, Robert Sebastian Thiel, Jessica Uhrig, Hong Yu, Warda Ahmed, Julie Even, Laura Haase, Corinna Holtwerth, Andreas Seiffert, Niels Thelen, Marten Urban

Exhibition preparation
Christian Werthmann, Evelyn König, Lisa Seiler, Joseph Claghorn, Marcus Hanke, Nina Dvorak

Scientific assistants
Sebastian Ballan, Leonie Wiemer, Johanna Jöcker, Julian Heikel, Ben Jamin Grau

Duration
2011–today

Alejandro Echeverri

The Colombian-German Collaboration between Urbam and ILA

The main focus of our work at Urbam, our Center for Urban and Environmental Studies at EAFIT University in Medellín, is the transformation and innovation of informal urbanization.

Our base, the city of Medellín, has a fundamental problem related to the informal occupancy in the slopes of the mountains in the northern parts of the city. The combination of geologically unstable soils, intense rainfall events, and unregulated housing construction is creating a life-threatening condition for large numbers of our low-income citizens. Solutions have to be found, not only for Medellín and the Aburrá Valley—urban landslides occur in many other Andean cities in Colombia—but also Latin America. On a worldwide scale, there were 2,662 landslides, with 32,322 casualties alone between 2004 and 2010. A number that is expected to increase through the further progression of climate change. Medellín seems to be a perfect laboratory for potential solutions not only because of the complexity and intensity of its problems, but also because of the proven capacity of its institutions and communities to engage complex situations. While the government of the city is applying Social Urbanism strategies that were initially developed and tested in other informal areas of the city, the fundamental problem of uncontrolled construction in risky areas could not be brought under control. Families are still constructing houses in the dangerous hills on an extensive scale.

In 2011 we decided at Urbam to collaborate with Professor Werthmann's team of landscape architects, first at Harvard Graduate School of Design then with the Institute of Landscape Architecture (ILA) at Hannover University in a two-phased project that eventually lasted three years. Our goal was to search for possibilities to innovate mitigation and anticipatory processes through community-based strategies. The focus was the neighborhoods that are susceptible to landslides in Medellín.

The first phase resulted in a regional study, considering the whole Aburrá Valley, the history and future of informal growth, and the location, history, and source of landslides. We concluded this study called, Rehabitar la Ladera, Shifting Ground, in 2012.

Furthermore, we continued with a more precise research project, which we called Rehabitar la Montaña, which finished by the end of 2013, where we studied two cases in detail, the neighborhoods of La Cruz and Honda, with 16,000 residents and 4,000 housing units. By observing the occupation process, working closely with the communities, and applying innovative green infrastructure solutions, we came up with five pilot projects. These are still in the process of validation and adoption by the government of Medellín based on a new collaborative relationship with local communities.

Urbam's knowledge of local conditions and experience of working with the communities in combination with the knowledge, methodology, and landscape expertise of the Hannover team, has allowed us to advance innovative approaches to these extreme problems that Urbam could not have developed on its own in this form. After five years of continued cooperation, both teams would agree that the acquisition of a truly happy and ultimately effective collaboration across the very real hardships of long travel distances, different time zones, dissimilar cultures, language barriers, and disciplinary views requires the build-up of trust and ultimately friendship. Based on this acquired trust, mutual respect, and friendship, we hope that we can test our approaches on the ground and deduct useful knowledge for the development of Medellín together, but also for other cities facing similar issues.

-

Christian Werthmann

São Paulo

10

São Paulo, Brasil
The Lost River of Tamanduateí

São Paulo is an endlessly fascinating city. Here, one
can study in detail the consequences of an extremely rapid wave of
urbanization, which is yet to reach other settlements in the world. This
experience is not always reassuring. The metropolis of twenty million
inhabitants is characterized to a great extent by social inequalities and
environmental problems. Solutions to structural problems such as
widespread poverty or large-scale flooding—in alternation with water
shortages—urgently need to be found. Here, however, São Paulo's fast
adaptability to possible change gives cause for hope. After 150 years
of rapid urbanization, urban growth has slowed, and planning authorities
are now seizing the historical opportunity to transform their city long
term.

◂   The Tamanduateí has been completely channeled and
    partially streamed through pipes since 1957, 2015

In this climate of radical change, our team was invited by the central planning authority, the Secretaria Municipal de Desenvolvimento Urbano (SMDU) under the direction of the architect Fernando de Mello Franco, to take a look at one of São Paulo's numerous rivers. In 2015 we did this over the course of one year along with several teachers and a total of thirty-five master's degree students from the Faculty of Architecture and Landscape of Leibniz Universität Hannover.

The river selected, the Tamanduateí, is a small but historically important, centrally located body of water; the river has been completely canalized, partially covered over, and is badly polluted. This is not unusual, since in the phase of industrialization, all of the rivers of the highland basin of São Paulo were channelized. This in turn has had decisive effects on São Paulo's current self-perception as a city. To be able to understand this one must examine the landscape origins of the Brazilian metropolis.

The Jesuits established São Paulo in 1554, far away from the colonial cities of the time. At that time it was an isolated outpost of civilization in a landscape of forests and small farmsteads, centered around a small monastery on a hilly highland plateau, some sixty kilometers away from the coast and 800 meters above sea level. The subtropical climate that prevails here, with an annual precipitation of up to 1,500 millimeters, continues to guarantee lush vegetation cover even today. At that time the hills were covered by dense Atlantic rainforest, with rivers, streams, and innumerable rivulets characterizing the valleys. The Tupi people called one of these many rivers the "Tamanduateí"—the river of the anteaters. For a long time, this only thirty-five-kilometer-long river served as part of the major transport route towards the coast in the southeast until a spectacular cog railway took over this function in 1866. At the end of the nineteenth century, then, the Tamanduateí served mainly as a place for recreation and bathing for the 30,000 residents of the small, up-and-coming city. Over the course of the next 150 years, however, this small city would grow seven-hundredfold to become one of the largest metropolises in the world, with over twenty million inhabitants in an area sprawling over 8,000 square kilometers. Millions of rural farmers were attracted by the expanding industries and moved to the city. Due to a lack of capital resources, they built their own housing settlements (favelas), mostly on rough terrain near the factories. In this unimaginable phase of growth, the rainforest—after the rivers, the second most important characteristic of the landscape—was chopped down, the farms disappeared, and, in the mid-twentieth century, all the rivers of the highland plateau, including the Tamanduateí, were channelized in order to create space for industries, railway lines, and major roads on the former floodplains. By the turn of the millennium, the city had grown so rapidly with a corresponding increase in impermeable surfaces, that the

▲ Fig tree on the bank of the Tamanduateí, ca. 1910

▼ The Tamanduateí River while only thirty-five kilometers long is nevertheless historically significant: São Paulo was established along this river in 1554

ndungskern
Metropole

sser einzugsgebiet
an luatei

Tietê

sse einzugsgebiet Tietê
er Metropole São Paulo

▼ After 1850, the Tamanduateí River served the city as a recreation zone, ca. 1910

channelized rivers were no longer able to drain the storm water runoff, which had increased many times over, causing low-lying parts of the city to flood on a regular basis.

In this process of urbanization, São Paulo lost both of its significant landscape characteristics—the rivers and the forests. Iconic images of the city typically show a sea of high-rise buildings. While the image, pride, and self-identity of many other metropolises is shaped by the charming interplay of landscape and city—Rio de Janeiro with its spectacular mountainous coast, San Francisco with its bay, or New York with its location on a peninsula, for instance—São Paulo has none of this, only buildings extending as far as the horizon. In a certain sense, then, São Paulo is the city of cities. Or as de Mello Franco pointedly put it: "Rio has the beach, we have nothing."

At the same time, the rivers are nevertheless very present in everyday life. The citizens of São Paulo orient themselves based on the rivers, along which all the major roads run. Framed by these multilane highways, inaccessible and polluted, the rivers and their banks nonetheless offer no reference points so as to trigger something resembling pride, let alone to be able to act as recreation areas. Today, now that São Paulo's growth has slowed, a change in thinking is taking place. People would very much like to reclaim the rivers again.

With this in mind, our team chose the lower course of the Tamanduateí, around which the city is planning a huge densification project, as a case study. The situation is complex and valuable with respect to the history of the city. The former floodplain is home to the oldest industrial area in Brazil and to São Paulo's oldest favela. When the Henry Ford industrial area was established in the 1920s, it was still located at the edge of the city, along the

The former flood plain is today filled with industry and self-constructed settlements (favelas), 2015

In the past thirty years, the Henry Ford industrial area has lost 50,000 industrial jobs. With 30,000 workplaces, it nevertheless remains an important employer in the heart of the city, 2015

Vila Prudente in the industrial area is the oldest favela in São Paulo, 2015

The favelas in the industrial area are characterized by an extremely high residential density, 2015

Tamanduateí, which had just been recently been channelized. One hundred years later, the approximately 300-hectare-large area, easily accessible and surrounded by dense housing areas, represents one of the most desirable areas for redevelopment in the center of the city. The city wants to retain the industrial uses of the area with its 30,000 workplaces, but double the population of the surrounding housing areas in order to enable more people, above all in lower income groups, to live and work in the city. Several smaller favelas are already situated directly in the industrial area, being settled on derelict industrial sites, including São Paulo's oldest favela, Vila Prudente, with some 1,600 dwellings. Attracted by the industrial jobs, the early arrivals built their settlement in a marsh directly next to the Tamanduateí. Today, the citizens of this residential district live in densely packed urban spaces characterized by an acute lack of publicly usable open space.

There is now a dire need for additional recreation areas for the long-standing and newly arrived residents. Unfortunately, the Tamanduateí is not able to offer anything in this respect. On the contrary, it continues to flow as a liquid central median of a multilane highway, heavily polluted, smelly, and inaccessible. When there are heavy rains, it occasionally escapes its bed to flood parts of the industrial district and surrounding favelas. The urban master plan, even with the enormous upheavals it envisions, deliberately ignores the Tamanduateí—its location between highways, railway lines, and industrial properties, whose value has meanwhile increased substantially, simply seems to be too hopeless, and the city permits hardly any possibilities for access (for instance, by means of expropriation).

In light of this situation, we challenged our students with an impossible question: Can a dead river, whose valley will soon accommodate over a quarter million individuals once again become a home to landscape?

The students reacted to this provocation with a spectrum of multiphase approaches, from small, quickly achievable changes in the existing riverbed to complex hydraulic and traffic-related restructurings. Supported by a water engineer, the proposals ranged from the relocation and reduction of roads at one extreme, to relocating the river itself, creating elongated flood parks, with new promenades and pedestrian bridges, as well as water-collecting streets and water-storing residential districts at the other. What became unambiguously clear in the process is that the river ultimately has to be given more space so as to ease flooding and increase the desirability of the space. It was also shown that the city has to develop cleansing and retention networks for rainwater in the city districts in order to absorb more storm water in the city while transferring less, but cleaner water to the rivers. The best of the student approaches were able to produce connections between the favelas, the industrial area, and the river. On the whole, they showed that it would be fundamentally possible to regain the river as a recreation and identity-forming space and to deal with water more sustainably.

An agreement had been reached with the municipal authorities that our proposals—despite the need to be closely anchored in reality—should not be too burdened by realization strategies and questions of political feasibility. Indeed, this is often a reason to invite a team from abroad: to have people who can look at a problem with "fresh" eyes and then perhaps come up with solutions that would not necessarily occur to local residents. In our case, we as teachers put a great emphasis on technical practicability—above all with respect to hydrology—while, for reasons of competence and complexity alone, financial aspects did not stand in the foreground. In a second step, the planning authority in São Paulo then checked the students' proposals for feasibility and practicability.

▶

The 320 square kilometer Tamanduateí Watershed is shared by six municipalities, 2016

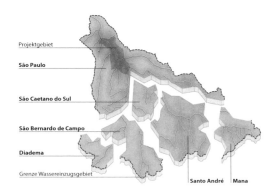

Projektgebiet

São Paulo

São Caetano do Sul

São Bernardo de Campo

Diadema

Grenze Wassereinzugsgebiet

Santo André   Mana

In the process, many of the proposals were identified as being worthwhile, but nevertheless politically difficult to realize. For example, in discussions of the students' proposals with São Paulo's planning authority, it became apparent that the critical relocation or narrowing of the highway along the river was regarded as being politically unfeasible. For the other measures, such as reclaiming land and relocating roads or the river, São Paulo would have to develop aggressive construction regulations and land redistribution and traffic management models, which are considered difficult to implement in the current political and economic climate. In this context, it should be noted that, at the time of the study in 2016, Brazil was in the middle of a serious economic and government crisis. The authorities listed only two legal instruments that seemed suitable for creating space for the river: the first is a national law that stipulates a minimum distance of at least fifty meters between physical structures and a river. Space could be created for the Tamanduateí in the long term if dilapidated buildings situated within this minimum distance were required to be demolished. It is, however, difficult to predict whether the application of the law would truly be enforced. This consequently means that it could potentially take a long time to assemble a con-nected sequence of properties. The second possibility is a financing instrument by means of which capital is raised by selling vertical building rights. With this capital, it would then be possible to pur-chase land to build parks along the Tamanduatéi. It is, however, not possible to foresee whether the money would actually be used for the river or whether it would be used instead for other public projects such as the urgent construction of schools or improving the public transportation infrastructure.

As is so often the case, it became clear that reclaiming the Tamanduateí as an identity-forming landscape element for São Paulo is not a question of technical or financial feasibility, but rather a question of the positioning of political objectives—a question of the priorities set by the elected representatives of the people.

The current state of the Tamanduateí makes it easy for these political representatives to remain idle. How is one supposed to set the energies and finances in motion to fight for access to a river that stinks, and that is indeed hazardous to people's health? Would it not be better to wait until the Tamanduateí has been cleaned up before spending money for riverbank promenades and river parks?

In our work focusing on the Tamanduateí, we came to the conviction that one should not wait for clean water, but instead make access to the dirty river now, since it is impossible to foresee when the water quality of the Tamanduateí will actually improve. Although the various jurisdictions that are located in the catchment area collectively agreed to clean the river long ago, up to now there has been no noticeable improvement in water quality.

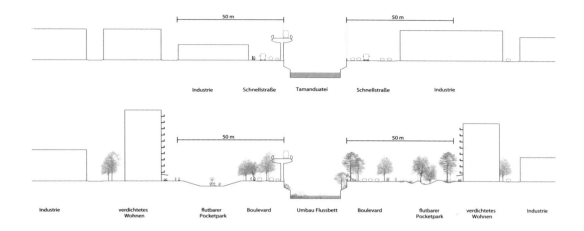

Industrie   Schnellstraße   Tamanduateí   Schnellstraße   Industrie

Industrie   verdichtetes Wohnen   flutbarer Pocketpark   Boulevard   Umbau Flussbett   Boulevard   flutbarer Pocketpark   verdichtetes Wohnen   Industrie

▲ According to a federal law, there should be no buildings closer than fifty meters to a river bank. Over a thirty year process the river edges could be reconstructed

▼ The course of the Tamanduateí was straightened while being channeled in the first half of the 20th century

▼ Potential transformation strategy: through the enforcement of the law, a series of floodable pocket parks could be constructed

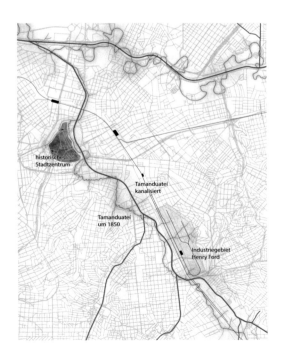

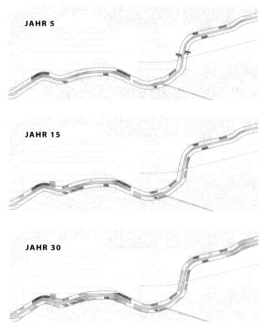

The current and future residents of the Tamanduateí valley, however, need spaces for rest and recreation now.

If the design of new recreation spaces remains decoupled from the river, as envisioned in the current master plan, the current "out of sight, out of mind" attitude toward the status quo of the Tamanduateí will be further cemented. Access to the water at the earliest possible point, in contrast, could perhaps speed up the water quality improvement process, as the residents of the valley—stimulated by the poor condition of the river which they can now more directly experience—would exert increased political pressure.

The case of the Tamanduateí touches on much broader issues. In a climate in which growth is slowing and the further development of public transportation is being planned, São Paulo's rivers, as ruined as they also are at the moment, offer a historic opportunity to let the historically characteristic landscape of the region to redefine the metropolis's sea of high-rise buildings, and to give the city's inhabitants an urban reserve. São Paulo's municipal authorities and planners are well aware of this and are wrestling in earnest with how they might improve the physical state of their rivers and their attractiveness as public spaces. They are prepared to engage in a long struggle.

•

Project data

Project title
São Paulo, Brazil—The Lost River of Tamanduateí

Project team
Institute for Landscape Architecture, Leibniz Universität Hannover: Christian Werthmann, Heike Schäfer, Marcus Hanke, Hinnerk Voermanek; Institute of Design and Urban Design, Leibniz University Hannover: Andreas Quednau, Frank Eittorf, Henning Dehn

Project type
academic study project of the Leibniz Universität Hannover

Cooperation partner
Secretaria Municipal de Desenvolvimento Urbano (SMDU), São Paulo: Fernando de Mello Franco, Giselle Mendonça, Kátia Canova, Gabriel Hollaender Vilela, Carolina Heldt, Alessandra Iturrieta, Tomás Wissenbach

Project advising
School of Architecture and Urbanism (FAUUSP), University of São Paulo: Alexandre Delijaicov, Paulo Pellegrino, Nabil Bonduki, Mariana Terra; São Paulo Urbanismo: Gustavo Partezani, Carla Poma, Rita Gonçalves, Marilena Fajersztajn, Melina Possagnolo, Thiago Carneiro, Robernize Chakour, Luciana Loureiro, Patricia Saran; André Delfino da Silva, local leadership; Francisco Parisi, superintendent at the commercial association

Students:

Master studio project The Lost River of Tamanduateí
Corinna Wassermann, Dantong Su, Elke Börner, Franziska Mzyk, Han Mei, Jeremy Brightman, Johanna Jöcker, Julia Schairer, Katharina Müller, Katja Richter, Leonie Wiemer, Marius Janning, Matthäus Würtz, Rodrigo Caracciolo Martins, Siyu Lin, Stefanie Rötemeier, Stephan Rost, Ting Bian, Wei Zheng, Xing Xu

Master's studio project Metroplitan Symbiosis
Ben Che, Xiaoli Chen, Sofia Hanina, Felicitas Höringklee, Hao Hu, Johanna Joecker, Clemens Langsiepen, Franziska Lesser, Johanna Leyh, Han Mai, Hung Trung Mai, Florian Reischer, Finn Dominik Schneck, René Stahl, Yujun Wang, Leonie Wiemer, Mengyao Xing, Hengyu Yang, Wie Zheng, Haixi Zhu

Master plan team of the Secretaria Municipal de Desenvolvimento Urbano (SMDU), São Paulo:

Project team
Fernando de Mello Franco: SP-Urbanismo Presidente, Gustavo Partezani: SP-Urbanismo executive design officer, Carla Poma: design manager, Marcelo Ignatios: structuring manager, Rita Cassia G S Goncalves: design leader

Urban design
Andrea de Oliveira Tourinho, Eduardo Tavares de Carvalho, Fernando Henrique Gasperini, Luciana Loureiro, Marcos Alexandre Leão Moraes, Marilena Fajersztajn, Maria Cristina Fernandes, Melina Giannoni de Araujo Possagnolo, Olga Maria Soares e Gross, Robernize Chakour, Thaisa Folgosi Froes, Waldir Macho La Rubbia

Economic analysis
Andre Fabiano Hoon Kwak, Antonio Jesus Galdiano Junior, Bruno de Lima Borges, Hyun In Ra, Ivan de Andrade Paixão, Thiago Antonio Pastorelli Rodrigues

Legal analysis
Jose Antonio Apparecido Junior

Social dialogue
Juliana Cipolletta: Comunicação, Patrícia Saran: Diálogo Social, Thomas Len Yuba: Comunicação

Contract management
Ricardo A. Grecco Teixeira, Ana Paula Roque de Sousa, Carla Raduan de Oliveira

Advisor
Consórcio CMVC: Hector Vigliecca e Associados; Astoc GmbH; WALM Engenharia e Contacto Consultores

Exhibition preparation
Christian Werthmann, Evelyn König, Lisa Seiler, Joseph Claghorn, Marcus Hanke, Heike Schäfer; scientific assistants: Sebastian Ballan, Leonie Wiemer, Johanna Jöcker, Julian Heikel, Ben Jamin Grau, Rodrigo Carraciola-Martins

Duration
2014–today

Fernando de Mello Franco, Rita Gonçalves

Neighborhoods of Tamanduateí

Between 2012 and 2015, the Municipality of São Paulo has developed a Master Plan for the neighborhoods along the river Tamanduateí. The starting points of this plan were two major aspects in the configuration of this territory: the river—since a great portion of this area is on the river's floodplain—and the railway, which follows the river's course.

The choice of the river as a central element brought up the discussions about flooding, drainage, and the poor condition of its edges, surrounded by an expressway system. The railway, in turn, raised the questions of industrial and railroad heritage, of the fragmented streets and the uncertainties about the future of the productive spaces nearby.

The plan remained in its scope: giving shape to the framework for the desired changes towards an environmental qualification, a friendly relationship between the city and its rivers, and a land use improvement to promote employment and affordable housing.

The plan also sets building regulations; defines places for productive activities, for new streets and pathways, and for new green areas connected with drainage structures; and finally, selects, among a wide range of needs, the interventions that could allow us to achieve the expected changes in the territory.

Conceived under the present conditions, the plan was targeted to exist for thirty years. This period will transform the horizon of expectations, in which we have laid down the plan's guidelines, goals, and solutions.

The students of Leibniz Universität Hannover have defined their project areas in the territory covered by the Master Plan, which had provided them with an overview of the general issues concerned.

As foreign students, they have patiently built up their own base of knowledge about the area they have chosen to study. They have gone through the history of urbanization to understand the economic and industrial development aspects that have formed that settlement. From this knowledge, the two questions that the projects aimed to answer have emerged: how to conciliate the needs of housing and industries and how to organize the expressway system to improve the quality of the river's waterfront.

The projects, which could be considered now as unlikely, or ambitious, have developed and subverted the original Master Plan, foreseeing the uture decades of its term. In any case, the projects do reveal possible realities, unconsidered due to the restraint of the former planners.

The students have conceived alternatives for the encapsulated river: in some cases the expressways are moved away from it, whereas in other projects, the river gets a new bed. In all the proposals, the city discovers its lost river, which opens itself into green terraces beyond its former channel. In these future scenes, not only the river, but also housing is improved, and the industrial heritage is redefined. People get closer to the waterfront, which isn't inhospitable anymore.

How do we imagine the rivers' future in São Paulo? We consider that many "lost" rivers in our city could benefit from this very hydrophilic design that guided the students' projects. Despite the huge limitations of restricted public funds, the predatory praxis of raw sewage discharge into water bodies is being reverted. There is a common understanding that rivers and streams shouldn't be laid between concrete walls anymore and that we must prevent rivers' surroundings from inadequate occupation. Maybe someday we ought to undo the past mistakes and renaturalize some of the rivers we have buried in the last hundred years.

It's valuable to imagine that unforeseen conditions could lead us to the solutions designed by the students from Leibniz Universität Hannover. This is the contribution of their foreign perspective: to reveal a range of possibilities that we have censored because we don't dare to think beyond the present contingencies.

OFICINAA

Silvia Benedito,
Alexander Häusler

From Dimness to Heightened Brightness: Fieldwork in the Museum

How to create an exhibition on landscape works where the modes of examination rely on the direct experience intrinsic to fieldwork? How to convey a sense of spatial immersion while delivering specialized information? Ultimately, how to capture the living and working practices of being out there? With attentive eyes and an investigative mind-set, the exhibition design emerges from questions of unfamiliarity and apprehension in outdoor landscapes. The design reflects on forensic journeys in global terrains for exploration and discovery—botanical, geological, social, cultural, and climatic. From the unfamiliar contexts of the out there to the localized knowledge acquired through working in the field and with communities, the audience—likewise the landscape architect—gradually enters into the landscapes of inquiry.

Treated as fieldwork in itself, the exhibition is an exploratory field where process, experiments, and evidence form the space of meandering.

The projects are explored through projective "action-offices" that evoke past exploratory and taxonomical enterprises. The space is darkened, the work emerging as focal points of apprehension and attention in the open field. The audience is invited to gather and explore materials, artefacts, and ideas as astronauts in outer space. Landscape includes other hues and worlds besides green, and from these spaces of immersive dimness emerges moments of heightened brightness.

View into the model of
the exhibition

Author Biographies

Alejandro Echeverri is a Colombian architect and the director of the Centro de Estudios Urbanos y Ambientales (urbam) at EAFIT University in Medellín.

Mohammed El Haddi is director in the Regional Authority of Agriculture of the Casablanca Region (Direction Régionale de l'Agriculture, DRA).

John Beardsley is the Director of Garden and Landscape Studies at Dumbarton Oaks Research Library and Collection in Washington D. C. Trained as an art historian, he is the author of numerous books on contemporary art and design, including *Earthworks and Beyond: Contemporary Art in the Landscape* (4th edition, 2006). Beardsley has taught in departments of landscape architecture at the University of Virginia, the University of Pennsylvania, and Harvard University.

Gerado Gazmuri is an architect and was Director of Construction, TECHO Haiti 2013 – 2015.

Undine Giseke is professor at Technische Universität Berlin, Chair of Landscape Architecture and Open Space Planning since 2003. In 1987 together with three further partners she founded bgmr landscape architects. She was director of the inter-and transdisciplinary research project Urban Agriculture as an Integrative Factor of Climate-Optimized Urban Development, Casablanca (UAC project) funded by the BMBF research program Future Megacities form 2005 to 2014. For her research and practice activities in 2015 she was awarded the Gottfried Semper Architecture Prize for Sustainable Planning and Construction.

Juliane Brandt is geographer, research associate, and doctoral candidate at the Chair of Landscape Architecture and Open Space Planning, Technische Universität Berlin. Research activity and coordination within the framework of BMBF projects Urban Agriculture Casablanca (UAC project) and Rapid Planning, research focus: transferability.

Azzedine Hafif is director in the Planning Authority of the Casablanca Region (Agence Urbaine de Casablanca, AUC).

Rita Cassia Gonçalves is a planner in the urban plannning department of São Paulo. She leads the design team for the urban redevelopment of the Tamanduateí Valley.

Johann-Christian Hannemann is research associate at the Chair of Landscape Architecture and Public Space, Professor Regine Keller, Technische Universität München. Holding a Master of Science in Urbanism and a Bachelor of Science in Landscape Architecture, since 2013/14 he coordinates the transdisciplinary research platform Urban Strategies for Onaville (Haiti).

Abdelkader Kaioua is director in the Regional Authority of Housing, Urbanism and Spatial Planning, Grand Casablanca (Inspection Régionale du Ministère de l'Habitat, de l'Urbanisme et de la Politque de la Ville, IRHUPV).

Christoph Kasper is landscape architect, research associate and lecturer and doctoral candidate at the Chair of Landscape Architecture and Open Space Planning, Technische Universität Berlin. Research activity and coordination within the framework of BMBF projects Urban Agriculture Casablanca (UAC project) and Rapid Planning, research focus: urban-rural linkages.

Regine Keller became a research associate at Technische Universität München in the Department of Landscape Architecture and Design in 1996. Before her present post, Professor Keller taught at Hochschule für angewandte Wissenschaften München. Since 2005 Regine Keller is Professor of Landscape Architecture and Public Space, Faculty of Architecture, Technische Universität München. She runs her own design studio Keller-Damm-Roser Landscape Architects and Urban Planners since 1998.

Andres Lepik is Director of Architekturmuseum and Professor for Architecture History and Curatorial Studies at Technische Universität München since 2012. From 2007 to 2010 he worked as Curator for Architecture at The Museum of Modern Art and was a Loeb Fellow at the Graduate School of Design, Harvard University in 2011.

Dihua Li is a landscape ecologist and Associate professor at the College of Architecture and Landscape Architecture at Peking University.

Fernando de Mello Franco is a Brazilian architect and was the director of urban planning department from 2013 to 2016 in São Paulo (Secretaria Municipal de Desenvolvimento Urbano).

Rosa Maria Miglio Toledo De Rodriguez is an agriculture engineer and professor at the National Agrarian University (UNALM) in Lima, Peru.

Abias Philippe Mumuhire is an architect in the Urban Planning and Urban Design Department at the City of Kigali (CoK).

Jörg Rekittke is Professor and Deputy Dean of Landscape Architecture, School of Architecture and Design, RMIT University, Melbourne. From 2009 to 2016, he was Associate Professor in the Master of Landscape Architecture Program, National University of Singapore. He also held positions at University of Wageningen and RWTH Aachen University.

Jürgen Renn is Director at the Max Planck Institute for the History of Science in Berlin, Honorary Professor at the Humboldt Universität zu Berlin and the Freie Universität Berlin as well as Adjunct Professor for Philosophy and Physics at Boston University. His research focuses on structural changes in systems of knowledge, particularly in the natural sciences. His research interests are longitudinal studies of the emergence and development of mechanical knowledge, history of ancient science, history of modern physics, history of the globalization of knowledge, comparative studies of science in Europe and China, historical epistemology, and the Digital Humanities.

Antje Stokman is Professor of Architecture and Landscape at HafenCity Universität Hamburg. From 2010–17, she was the Director of the Institute of Landscape Planning and Ecology at the Faculty of Architecture and Urban Planning, Universität Stuttgart. Before that, she was assistant professor at Leibniz Universität Hannover from 2005–2010. She is a practicing landscape architect and member of Studio Urbane Landschaften, Hamburg since 2010.

Christian Werthmann is a Professor at the Institute of Landscape Architecture, Leibniz Universität Hannover. He researches the threats and potential of landscape in low income neighborhoods—a line of research that he initiated at the Harvard Graduate School of Design. His latest co-authored book (with Jessica Bridger), *Metropolis Nonformal*, gives an overview of 25 expert approaches for self-built urbanization.

Sarah Westropp is the owner of the Bobocha Resort on Siladen Island, North Sulawesi, Indonesia.

Kathrin Wieck is a landscape architect with a doctoral degree and research associate and lecturer at the Chair of Landscape Architecture and Open Space Planning, Technische Universität Berlin. Research activity within the framework of BMBF project Urban Agriculture Casablanca (UAC project), coordination of UAC publication, research focus: production of space and urban informality.

Kongjian Yu is the founder and Dean of College of Architecture and Landscape Architecture at Peking University and the founder and President of Turenscape, Beijing.

Daniel Zarza is Professor of Urbanism, Universidad de Alcalá, Madrid.

Literature

Casablanca, Morocco, p. 20

Undine Giseke,
Kathrin Wieck,
Christoph Kasper

- AUC (Agence urbaine de Casablanca)/IAURIF (Institut d'aménagement et d'urbanisme de la Région Ile-de-France) *Plan de développement stratégique et schéma directeur de l'aménagement urbain de la Wilaya de la Région du grand Casablanca (SDAU), Rapport justificatif,* Kigali (2008).
- Brown, Valerie A., Harris, John A., and Russel, Jaqueline Y. *Tackling Wicked Problems: Through the Transdisciplinary Imagination,* New York (2010).
- Giseke, U., M. Gerster-Bentaya, F. Helten, M. Kraume, D. Scherer, G. Spars, A. Adidi, F. Amraoui, S. Berdouz, M. Chlaida, M. Mansour, and M. Mdafai (eds.) *Urban Agriculture for Growing City Regions: Connecting Urban-Rural Spheres in Casablanca,* Oxon, Abingdon, New York (2015).

Statement, Stimulating Change in Institutional Practices, p. 33

Azzedine Hafif,
Abdelkader Kaioua,
Mohammed El Haddi

- A. Adidi, Y. Moustanjidi, M. El Haddi, A. Kaioua, and A. Hafif (2015), "F1 Strategies and actions: F1.3 Stimulating change in institutional practices: Administration interfaces," in: U. Giseke et al. (eds.), *Urban Agriculture for Growing City Regions. Connecting Urban-Rural Spheres in Casablanca,* Oxon, Abingdon, New York, pp. 452–55.

Kigali, Rwanda, p. 36

Undine Giseke,
Juliane Brandt,
Christoph Kasper

- City of Kigali (2013) *Kigali City Master Plan Report*
- Kabalisa, Vincent de Paul. "Analyse contextuelle en matière de Gestion Intégrée des Ressources en Eau au Rwanda.," *Document de travail pour l'ONGProtos. Rapport definitive,* Kigali (2006).
- Kersting, Philippe. "Geomorphologische Untersuchungen im Land der tausend Hügel – oder: Wie europäisch ist die rwandische Landschaftsentwicklung?" *Forum ifl Heft,* 13, Leibniz-Institut für Länderkunde, Leipzig (2010).
- Manirakiza, Vincent. "Processus d'urbanisation de la ville de Kigali." *Rwanda: relation entre la dynamique spatiale et démographique,.* Chaire Quételet, Centre d'études du développement, Louvain-la-Neuve (2011), pp. 1–17: https://www.uclouvain.be/cps/ucl/doc/demo (accessed May 7, 2016).

Cañada Real Galiana, Spain, p. 48

Regine Keller

- Alberti, Leon Battista. "De pictura-1435," in: *Liber Liber.* Cecil Grayson, June 7, 1998. http://www.liberliber.it/mediateca/libri/a/alberti/de_pictura/html/libro03.htm (accessed April 2016).
- Dietz, Charlotte. *Leben neben der Abrißbirne.* (ed.) *Stern* (2014). August. (1) http://www.stern.de/politik/ausland/groesster-slum-europas-cañada-real-leben-neben-der-abrissbirne-3632530.html (accessed April 2016).
- Fidel, Enrique. *Ciudad Lineal de Arturo Soria* (2008). https://urbancidades.wordpress.com/2008/10/18/ciudad-lineal-de-arturo-soria/ (accessed April 30, 2016).

- Simone, AbdouMaliq. "People as infrastructure," in: Public Culture, (2014), pp. 407–429.
- Zarza, Daniel. *Un proyecto para la Cañada* (2011).

Statement, Livestock Drove Roads, p. 58

Daniel Zarza

- Eda Schaur, Ungeplante Siedlungen/*Non-Planned Settlements,* Publications of the Institute for Lightweight Structures, IL 39, Universität Stuttgart, ed. by Frei Otto
- Julius Klein, *The Mesta: A Study in Spanish Economic History, 1273–1836,* Cambridge, MA, 1920; new ed. Port Washington, NY, 1964.
- *La Mesta,* Madrid 1979 (= Colección Alianza Universidad).
- Daniel Zarza, "Flecos/ Fringe," in: *Fisuras* (May 1977), pp. 38–39.
- Daniel Zarza, "Que hacer en la Cañada?," in: *Proyecto Cañada* (Madrid 2010): http:// www.proyectocañada. es/2010/09 (accessed January 28, 2016).
- Daniel Zarza, "Ley Regional [para la Desafección de la Cañada Real Galiana], y swing de la Presidenta [...]," in: *Proyecto Cañada* (Madrid 2011): http:// www.proyectocañada. es/ley-regional-para-la-desafeccion-de-la-canada-real-galiana-con-swing-de-la-presidenta-lanzando-el-problema-social-real-a-los-ayuntamientos (accessed January 28, 2016).
- Daniel Zarza, "Proyectocañadaes," in: *Proyecto Cañada* (Madrid) 2012: http:// www.proyectocañada. es/2012/04 (accessed January 28, 2016).

Canaan, Haiti, p. 62

Johann-Christian Hannemann

- Ayiti Kale Je, Haiti Grassroots Watch. "Reconstruction's Massive Slum Will Cost 'Hundreds Of Millions,'" 2013. http://www. haitigrassrootswatch. com/journal/2013/6/17/ bidonville-coutera-des-centaines-de-millions-slum-will-cost.html (accessed Nov/08/2016).
- Mars, Kettly. *Vor dem Verdursten.* Trier: Litradukt. Literatureditionen Manuela Zeilinger-Trier, 2013.
- Hannemann, Johann-Christian, Christian Werthmann, and Thomas Hauck. "Designing for Uncertainty: The Case of Canaan, Haiti," in: D. Czechowski, T. Hauck, G. Hausladen (eds.), *Revising Green Infrastructure: Concepts Between Nature and Design,* Boca Raton, November 2014, pp. 323–351.
- Heimhuber, Valentin, Johann-Christian Hannemann, and Wolfgang Rieger. "Flood Risk Management in Remote and Impoverished Areas—A Case Study of Onaville, Haiti," in: *Water* 2015, 7(7), 3832–3860; doi:10.3390/w7073832; Special Issue *Sustainable Water Management and Decision Making under limited Data Availability.* http:// www.mdpi.com/2073-4441/7/7/3832/pdf (accessed Nov/08/2016).

Statement, Experiences of Participation in Haiti, p. 73

Gerardo Gazmuri

- https://www.techo. org/en-tu-pais/haiti-nomaspobreza/ (accessed November 29, 2016). (Official TECHO page; Haiti and the importance of volunteering.)
- https://ejempla.com/ actualidad/haiti-se-sigue-levantando-luego-del-terremoto (accessed November 29, 2016). (Short description of the current situation in the communities where TECHO has been working.)
- https://www.youtube.com/ watch?v=ASIDpV6QGeg (accessed November 29, 2016). (Video of the inauguration of the school in Gariche Prince.)
- http://www. elnuevoherald.com/ noticias/sur-de-la-florida/ article8964935.html (accessed November 29, 2016). (Newspaper article on funding campaign and plight of the communities.)
- http://www.haitilibre. com/en/news-15299-haiti-social-dhl-installs-solar-street-lights-and-plant-trees.html (accessed November 29, 2016). (Newspaper article on the Onaville street lighting installation project.)
- http://www.inducar.pt/ cp/ow_userfiles/plugins/ forum/attachment_44_ 507eea1fe8529.pdf (accessed November 29, 2016). (PDF Guide/manual on the methodologies of participative rural diagnostics on which TECHO-Haiti's experience was based.)
- http://www.gloobal.net/ iepala/gloobal/fichas/ ficha.php?entidad= Metodologias&id=1& opcion=descripcion# ficha_gloobal (accessed November 29, 2016). (More reference material on participative rural diagnostics.)

Bali, Indonesia, p. 76

Jörg Rekittke

- Russel Wallace, Alfred. *The Malay Archipelago: The Land of the Orang-Utan and the Bird of Paradise* (Stanfords Travel Classics), Oxford, 2016.
- Seidl, Ulrich. *Paradise: Love* (Movie), Ulrich Seidl Film, Austria, 2012.
- Rekittke, Jörg and Yazid Ninsalam, "Sliced Ecosystem: Modelling Transects of Vulnerable Marine Landscapes," in: *Journal of Digital Landscape Architecture,* Wichmann, Berlin, Offenbach, Issue 01 (2016), pp. 36–45.

Jakarta, Indonesia, p. 86

Jörg Rekittke

- Silver, Christopher. *Planning the Megacity: Jakarta in the Twentieth Century,* Abingdon/ Oxfordshire, 2008.
- Texier, Pauline. "Floods in Jakarta: When the Extreme Reveals Daily Structural Constraints and Mismanagement," *Disaster Prevention and Management,* 17/3, 2008, pp. 358–72.
- Rekittke, Jörg. "Being in Deep Urban Water. Finding the Horizontal Urban Trim Line, Jakarta, Indonesia," in: *Water Urbanisms East. Emerging Practices and Age-Old Traditions,* Kelly Shannon, Bruno de Meulder, eds., UFO Explorations of Urbanism Vol. 3, Park Books, Zurich, 2013, pp. 80–91.

Changde, China, p. 96

Antje Stokman

- Yu; Kongjian, Zhang, Lei; Li, Dihua. "Living with Water: Flood Adaptive Landscapes in the Yellow River Basin of China," in: *JoLa Journal of Landscape Architecture,* autumn 2008.
- Zheng, Nengshi. Wetland Park Xiajiadang, Changde Hannover: Unpublished Diploma thesis (2008).
- Zhu, Yingying. Grüne Infrastruktur und Freiraumgestaltung. Umgestaltung der Mischwassersammelbecken in der Stadt Changde Hannover: Unpublished Diploma thesis (2007).
- Changde Municipality (2015): Changde to Build a Sponge City. http://eng.changde.gov.cn/art/2015/4/29/art_66149_1601825.html (accessed 11/02/2016).

Lima, Peru, p. 110

Antje Stokman

- Stokman, Antje. "Clean Urbanism vs. Dirty Design: Appropriating Water Infrastructure Systems as Urban Water Landscapes," in: *South Architecture,* Vol. 1, No. 4 (2015), pp. 72–77
- Stokman, Antje; Poblet, R.; Nemcova, E. "Multidisciplinary Research/ Design/Build Summer Schools: Solutions for a Water scarce Future in Metropolitan Lima, Perú," in: Mahrin, B. (ed.): *Capacity Development Approaches for Future Megacities.* Book Series Future Megacities Vol. 3. Berlin (2014), pp. 106–122.
- Eisenberg, B.; Nemcova, E., Poblet, R.; Stokman, A. "Lima: a Megacity in the Desert/Lima: Lower Chillón River Plan/Lima: Integrated Urban Planning," in: Pahl-Weber, E.; Schwartze, F. (eds.): *Space Planning and Design. Integrated Planning and Design Solutions for Future Megacities.* Book Series Future Megacities Vol. 5. Berlin (2014), pp. 27–34, 79–88, 139–165.

- Nemcova, E.; Eisenberg, B., Poblet, R., Stokman, A. "Water-Sensitive Design of Open Space Systems. Ecological Infrastructure Strategy for Metropolitan Lima," in: Czechowski/ Hauck/Hausladen (eds.): *Revising Green Infrastructure: Concepts Between Nature and Design.* London (2014), pp. 357–387.
- Eisenberg, B.; Nemcova, E., Poblet, R.; Stokman, A. "Lima Ecological Infrastructure Strategy (LEIS). Integrated Urban Planning and Design Tools for a Water Scarce City." (2014). https://issuu.com/ilpe/docs/lima_ecological_infrastructure_stra_9c435aba38df2f (Zugriff 08.11.2016).
- Stokman, Antje; Jörg, J. "Strategic approaches to urban wetlands: Reconciling Nature Conservation, Engineering and Landscape Architecture," in: *Landscape Architecture Frontiers Magazine,* China (2013), pp. 44–55.
- Stokman, Antje. "Lima – Beyond the Park," in: *Topos 81, Water Landscapes* (2012), pp. 102–109.

Statement, Lessons from the Children's Park, p. 120

Rosa Maria Miglio Toledo De Rodriguez

- This article is based on the following paper: Miglio, Rosa; Garcia, Alexandra; Nemcova, Eva; Poblet, Rossana. "Water Sensitive Urban Design for Metropolitan Lima, Peru – 'Wastewater Treatment Park' – Application of Vertical Flow Constructed Wetlands in Public Open Space for Reuse of Treated Wastewater (Peru)," in: Hettiarachchi, Hiroshan; Ardakanian, Reza (eds.): *Safe Use of Wastewater in Agriculture: Good Practice Examples* (2016). Dresden, Germany: United Nations University, UNU-FLORES.

https://flores.unu.edu/wp-content/uploads/2016/08/Safe-Use-of-Wastewater-in-Agriculture-by-Hettiarachchi-Ardakanian.pdf (accessed 11/03/2016).
- Eisenberg, Bernd, Nemcova, Eva; Poblet, Rossana; Stokman, Antje. "Lima Ecological Infrastructure Strategy: Integrated urban planning strategies and design tools for water-scarce cities," (2014). Stuttgart, Germany: Institute of Landscape Planning and Ecology. https://issuu.com/ilpe/docs/lima_ecological_infrastructure_stra_9c435aba38df2f (German Version, accessed 11/03/2016). https://issuu.com/ilpe/docs/leis__-_esp_20141117_copy (Spanish Version, accessed 11/03/2016).
- Kosow, Hannah, León, Christian; Schütze, Manfred. "Escenarios para el futuro – Lima y Callao 2040," (2013): http://www.lima-water.de/documents/scenariobrochure.pdf (Spanish Version, accessed 11/03/2016).

Medellín, Colombia, p. 124

Christian Werthmann

- Claghorn, Joseph, Francesco Maria Orsini, Carlos Alejandro Echeverri Restrepo, and Christian Werthmann. "Rehabitar la Montaña: strategies and processes for sustainable communities in the mountainous periphery of Medellín," in: *urbe 8 (1)* (2016).

- Claghorn, Joseph, and Christian Werthmann. "Shifting Ground: Landslide Risk Mitigation through Community-Based Landscape Interventions," in: *Journal of Landscape Architecture* 10 (2015), pp. 6–15.

- Claghorn, Joseph, and Christian Werthmann. "Non-formal Growth and Landslide Risk. Strategies to improve non-formal settlements in Medellin," in: *TOPOS 90* (2015), pp. 50–56.
- Petley, David, 2012, "Global patterns of loss of life from landslides," in: *Geology,* vol. 40, no. 10, pp. 927–30.
- Werthmann, Christian, and Alejandro Echeverri, eds. *Rehabitar La Montaña: Estrategias y procesos para un hábitat sostenible en las laderas de Medellín.* Medellin: Universidad EAFIT, 2013.
- Werthmann, Christian, Alejandro Echeverri, and Ana Elvira Vélez, eds. *Rehabitar La Ladera: Shifting Ground.* Medellin: Universidad EAFIT, 2012. http://issuu.com/werthmann/docs/shifting-ground (accessed July 4, 2016).
- Werthmann, Christian, and Jessica Bridger, *Metropolis Nonformal.* San Francisco: Applied Research + Design Publishing, 2015.

São Paulo, Brasil, p. 136

Christian Werthmann

- Werthmann, Christian, and Jessica Bridger, *Metropolis Nonformal.* San Francisco (2015).
- Werthmann, Christian. "Pollution and Propaganda," in: *Design in the Terrain of Water,* (eds.) Anuradha Mathur and Dilip da Cunha, 123–29. Philadelphia (2014).
- Werthmann, Christian, ed. *Tactical Operations in the Informal City.* São Paulo: São Paulo Housing Agency, 2009.

Image Credits

Changde, China
- P. 96: © Lothar Fuchs
- P. 98: Graphic: © Antje Stokman
- P. 99.1: © Antje Stokman
- P. 99.2: © Antje Stokman
- P. 99.3: Graphic: © Nengshi Zheng
- P. 100.1: © Antje Stokman
- P. 100.2: © Antje Stokman
- P. 100.3: © Antje Stokman
- P. 100.4: Graphic: © Wasser Hannover
- P. 101: Graphic: © Wasser Hannover
- P. 102.1: © Lothar Fuchs
- P. 102, 103: © Lothar Fuchs
- P. 103 (right): © Lothar Fuchs
- P. 104: © Lothar Fuchs
- P. 105: © Lothar Fuchs

Statement: The Dream of Sponge Cities Is Starting to Become True
- P. 108: © Turenscape, Peking
- P. 109: © Turenscape, Peking

Lima, Peru
- P. 110: © Evelyn Merino-Reyna, Lima
- P. 112: © Marius Ege
- P. 113: © Evelyn Merino-Reyna, Lima
- P. 114.1 (top left): © Marius Ege
- P. 114, 115: © Marius Ege
- P. 114.2 (bottom left): © Andrea Balestrini
- P. 114.3 (bottom right): © Antje Stokman
- P. 116.1: © Maximilian Mehlhorn
- P. 116.2: © Maximilian Mehlhorn
- P. 116.3: © Rossana Poblet
- P. 116.4: © Rossana Poblet
- P. 116.5: © Antje Stokman
- P. 117.1: Graphic: © Eva Nemcova
- P. 117.2 (middle left): © Evelyn Merino Reyna
- P. 117.3 (middle right): © Marius Ege
- P. 117.4 (bottom left): © Eva Nemcova
- P. 117.5 (bottom right): © Andrea Balestrini
- P. 118: Graphic: © Marius Ege

Statement: Lessons from the Children´s Park
- P. 121.1: © Evelyn Merino Reyna
- P. 121.2: © Eva Nemcova
- P. 122.1: © Alexandra Garcia
- P. 122.2: © Alexandra Garcia

Medellín, Colombia
- P. 124: © Marcus Hanke, Institute for Landscape Architecture, Leibniz Universität Hannover
- P. 127.1 (top left): Source: Institute of Landscape Architecture, Leibniz Universität Hannover (ILA, LUH)/Centro de Estudios Urbanos y Ambientales (urbam)/Escuela de Administración, Finanzas e Instituto Tecnológico, University of Medellín (EAFIT), based on CAD data of the City of Medellín
- P. 127.2 (top right): Image source: © Institute for Landscape Architecture, Leibniz Universität Hannover (ILA, LUH)/Centro de Estudios Urbanos y Ambientales (urbam)/Escuela de Administración, Finanzas e Instituto Tecnológico, Universität Medellín (EAFIT)
- P. 127.3: © Joseph Claghorn, Institute for Landscape Architecture, Leibniz Universität Hannover
- P. 128.1: Image source: © Marcus Hanke, Institute for Landscape Architecture, Leibniz Universität Hannover
- P. 128.2: Image source: © Institute for Landscape Architecture, Leibniz Universität Hannover (ILA, LUH)/Centro de Estudios Urbanos y Ambientales (urbam)/Escuela de Administración, Finanzas e Instituto Tecnológico, Universität Medellín (EAFIT)
- P. 128.3: Image source: © Institute for Landscape Architecture, Leibniz Universität Hannover (ILA, LUH)/Centro de Estudios Urbanos y Ambientales (urbam)/Escuela de Administración, Finanzas e Instituto Tecnológico, Universität Medellín (EAFIT)
- P. 130.1: Image source: © Institute for Landscape Architecture, Leibniz Universität Hannover (ILA, LUH)
- P. 130.2: Image source: © Institute for Landscape Architecture, Leibniz Universität Hannover (ILA, LUH)/Centro de Estudios Urbanos y Ambientales (urbam)/Escuela de Administración, Finanzas e Instituto Tecnológico, Universität Medellín (EAFIT)
- P. 131.1: Image source: © Institute for Landscape Architecture, Leibniz Universität Hannover (ILA, LUH)
- P. 131.2: Image source: © Institute for Landscape Architecture, Leibniz Universität Hannover (ILA, LUH)/Centro de Estudios Urbanos y Ambientales (urbam)/Escuela de Administración, Finanzas e Instituto Tecnológico, Universität Medellín (EAFIT)
- P. 132: Image source: © Institute for Landscape Architecture, Leibniz Universität Hannover (ILA, LUH)/Centro de Estudios Urbanos y Ambientales (urbam)/Escuela de Administración, Finanzas e Instituto Tecnológico, Universität Medellín (EAFIT)

São Paulo, Brasil
- P. 136: © Marcus Hanke, Institute for Landscape Architecture, Leibniz Universität Hannover
- P. 139.1: Image source: © Vincenzo Pastore, courtesy Instituto Moreira Salles, São Paulo
- P. 139.2: Image source: © on the basis of information Secretaria Municipal de Desenvolvimento Urbano (SMDU), São Paulo/drawing modified by the Institute for Landscape Architecture, Leibniz Universität Hannover
- P. 139.3: © Vincenzo Pastore, courtesy Instituto Moreira Salles, São Paulo
- P. 140.1: © Marcus Hanke, Institute for Landscape Architecture, Leibniz Universität Hannover
- P. 140.2: © Marcus Hanke, Institute for Landscape Architecture, Leibniz Universität Hannover
- P. 140.3: © Marcus Hanke, Institute for Landscape Architecture, Leibniz Universität Hannover
- P. 140.4: © Marcus Hanke, Institute for Landscape Architecture, Leibniz Universität Hannover
- P. 141: Graphic: © Institute for Landscape Architecture, Leibniz Universität Hannover, 2016
- P. 143.1: Image source: © Institute for Landscape Architecture, Leibniz Universität Hannover
- P. 143.2 (left bottom): Image source:: © on the basis of information from the Secretaria Municipal de Desenvolvimento Urbano (SMDU), São Paulo/drawing modified by the Institute for Landscape Architecture, Leibniz Universität Hannover/ historical map material
- P. 143.3 (right bottom): Image source: © Institute for Landscape Architecture, Leibniz Universität Hannover, based on CAD data of the City of São Paulo

From Dimness to Heightened Brightness— Fieldwork in the Museum
- P. 148, 149: © OFICINAA, Silvia Benedito, Alexander Häusler
- P. 149 (bottom): © OFICINAA, Silvia Benedito, Alexander Häusler

This book is published
in conjunction with
the exhibition:

out there

Landscape Architecture
on Global Terrain

Architekturmuseum
der TU München,
Pinakothek der Moderne
April 27 – August 20, 2017